To My

I HOPE ONE DAY I GET
TO PERSONALLY SHOW
YOU HOW THE "IMPOSSIBLE"
IS MADE POSSIBLE ...
WE DO RECOVER !

♡ ; PRAYER

B

# OUT OF THE GHETTO

A Journey from Addiction to a New Way of Being

## SEAN HARRISON

ARCHWAY
PUBLISHING

Archway Publishing books may be ordered through booksellers or by contacting:

Archway Publishing
1663 Liberty Drive
Bloomington, IN 47403
www.archwaypublishing.com
844-669-3957

ISBN: 978-1-4808-9955-1 (sc)
ISBN: 978-1-4808-9956-8 (hc)
ISBN: 978-1-4808-9957-5 (e)

Library of Congress Control Number: 2020922614

Print information available on the last page.

Archway Publishing rev. date: 04/16/2021

I dedicate this book to my dear mother, who never gave up on me. I hope I made you proud.

# FOREWORD

*by Peter Bolland*

IN GREEK MYTHOLOGY, PERSEPHONE WAS THE GODDESS of the underworld, but not by choice. One day while picking flowers alongside a beautiful stream, her evil uncle Hades grabbed her and dragged her down into his realm – the underworld. And there she stayed.

Meanwhile, her mother, Demeter, searched for her lost daughter. But even an Earth Mother Goddess as powerful as Demeter failed. As she sank into despair, the whole world withered with her.

Something had to be done. Persephone's father Zeus intervened, ordering his brother Hades to release her. But Hades, being the crafty bastard that he was, struck a deal. Persephone had to eat a magic pomegranate seed. As in agricultural mythologies the world over, the seed represents the unbroken circle between life and death, for it is in the death-stage of any plant that it goes to seed. When she emerged from hell, the whole world was reborn with her, much to her mother's delight. The two reunited, and nature's generative power was renewed. But the underworld, and Hades, never completely released their grip – she had to spend half of every year there. That was the price of her freedom. Like Persephone, we all carry our trauma with us and find a way to bloom in spite of it.

If Zeus and Demeter are the male-female masks of divinity, with their infinitely life-giving powers, then Persephone is us – a child wandering the beautiful world, picking flowers, unaware of the dangers lurking just beneath the pleasures of life. Persephone's story reminds us that no matter how bad things get, there is always the possibility of renewal. For centuries, the ancient Greeks celebrated the story of Demeter and Persephone every year when the fallow darkness of winter gave way to the bounteous rebirth of spring.

The bottom line? We always underestimate ourselves. No matter how lost we feel, even when things are at their worst, there is an undeniable life-force surging through everything, including us. Don't bet against rebirth. It's as unstoppable as spring.

In Sean Harrison's harrowing memoir Out of the Ghetto, we're strapped into the first car on a rickety roller coaster ride through the streets of New York, poverty, addiction, and ultimately, triumph. It is a story at once uniquely specific and utterly universal. To anyone who, like Persephone, became mesmerized by the pretty flowers growing alongside the stream of life, Harrison's story rings true. Everyone will see themselves in this story, no matter where you grew up, and no matter how well (or otherwise) you navigated the youthful world of chemical adventuring.

But this is not just another addiction memoir. Harrison mercifully spares us most of the grimmer details of the abyss of addiction – enough said – and spends most of his time chronicling the rebirth that follows. That's what makes this book unique and inspirational – its boundless optimism and faith – faith in the sacred nature of the universe itself that bends toward healing, leans toward transcendence and rewards the struggle with wisdom.

Turning pain into purpose – that's what molds the bricks that pave the road out of purgatory. And through the hard labor and unearned grace of the recovery process, the road gets built one brick at a time. Then, with the help of the fellowship, the journey unfolds – the journey back to oneself. And that's perhaps the greatest achievement of this book, that in turning pain into purpose, Harrison models for all of us the sacred power of suffering – that like a forge, suffering is where the raw materials of our foundering psyche are melded into integrity, balance, harmony, and insight. As the first-century Roman Stoic philosopher Epictetus reminds us, "The trials we endure introduce us to our strengths."

Harrison is an apt student. He wields all he's learned into a synthesized narrative, drawing water from many wells – psychology, philosophy, spirituality, and the school of hard knocks. Maybe you weren't a drug courier for gangsters; maybe you didn't shoot dope into your vein in your mom's bathroom; maybe you didn't run in terror from the bullets of a speed-addled wise guy firing more for fun than malice – but you'll still see yourself in this harrowing but ultimately humane memoir.

In the end, this is a spiritual book. It is a book about wisdom. It is a book about finding the road back to life through the foggy paradox of egotism and self-doubt that plagues every addict. Even if you're never wrestled with drug or alcohol addiction, these maladies are a mirror held up to all of us, for we are all, by virtue of being human, prone to obsession, attachment, self-loathing, grandiosity, and selfishness – the building blocks of all compulsive disorders. In that sense, this book is about us – at our worst and our best. It is about the traps that ensnared us and the blades of discernment that cut us free. It is about the loneliness of never knowing where you belong and the homecoming in the sangha of your fellow seekers. It is about the ugliness of self-will run riot and the sublime clarity of spiritual humility. It is about the sadness of the wounds that can never be healed and the joyful surrender into the knowing that we are not defined by our wounds, healed or not.

In the end, wisdom and freedom mean the same thing. You cannot have one without the other. Wisdom is difficult to define. But freedom simply means relinquishing the illusion that you're in control. Instead of trying to run your life, you fall into partnership with your life, knowing that Life belongs to no one, is no one's property, and is a gift you only get to keep if you let go of it. Empowerment and powerlessness, victory and surrender, renunciation, and abundance – these paradoxes are at the heart of the awakened life, and this book gets at that wild, beating heart. Don't let this glimpse of awakening pass you by.

Peter Bolland is the Chair of the Philosophy and Humanities Department at Southwestern College in Chula Vista, California. Learn more at peterbolland.com

I WANT FIRST TO ACKNOWLEDGE THAT AMAZING grace, everywhere present, that saved a soul like me. I want to thank my family, especially my two incredible children, for coping with my OCD over the six years it took to complete this project. You have allowed me to experience love more profoundly than I ever dreamed possible.

To my spiritual teachers, past and present, for keeping me upright when the whole world seemed upside down. Without you, there would be no me. And kudos to my skilled physicians who keep this body, mind, and spirit thriving.

Salutations to my gifted photographer who made my photoshoot fun and my teeth whiter than they have ever been in my life. And to my tenacious troubleshooter for her creativity and perseverance in attaining the contractual agreements with Archway Publishing. A special shout out to my consigliere at Archway for her gentle non-ego deflating guidance.

I thank everyone who contributed your patience, time, talent, and constructive criticisms along the way. Finally, I want to acknowledge my new spirited psycho pug, who has given me a renewed purpose in life, free from the illusion there is such a state called retirement.

# INTRODUCTION

WOULD YOU ALLOW ANYONE YOU KNOW, OR SHOULD I say think you know, to walk through the corridors of your mind unabated, having the ability to peek into every dark corner they may find? It is always an honor and a privilege when asked to participate in another soul's awakening, one who found the courage to seek the truth of who they are without the masks or pretenses.

In writing these memoirs, fear became the dominant force of my thoughts. My concern comes not from who I am today but from the person I was in the past. It seemed like I was playing a leading role in an Alfred Hitchcock movie, moving from one nightmare to the next. Today, only a handful of people know what you are about to discover in these writings.

I have worked diligently to bury this story deep within the inner confines of my mind, leaving all my friends, neighbors, coworkers, as well as my wife and children without a clue of my previous existence. My fear has always been the same: If they ever discover the darkness within my past, they will never see me in the same light again.

These writings will come as a complete surprise to many of my esteemed colleagues in the medical community. In this small, interconnected society, the physicians I worked with trusted me not only with their careers but with their patients' health and well-being.

In 1982, I miraculously completed my studies at one of the most prestigious medical centers in New York City. For three decades, I have worked in a profession where I have excelled and provided my family with a lifestyle I never dreamed possible. It is a far cry from my senior year of high school when my classmates voted me as "The most likely to be dead by the time he's thirty."

Why *Out of the Ghetto*? As you continue to read, the "why" will speak for itself. The reader should be aware this book is not about any geographical change but about a dramatic shift in consciousness, from an inner-ghetto mentality to a new way of being. It is my hope you will not only read *Out of the Ghetto* but experience it for yourself.

# 1

# ALPHA BITS AND PIECES

IN THIS BOOK, I TELL TALES THAT ENCOMPASS MORE than half a century. However, the concept for *Out of the Ghetto* only began to take root on May 31, 2011. On that day, I got called back to my doctor's office to review what I thought would be a routine chest x-ray taken a few hours prior. In the previous six weeks, I unintentionally lost a total of twenty-one pounds, about 9 % of my body weight. I also developed excruciating right-sided chest pain and a cough that just would not quit.

Earlier that morning, while assisting in surgery, I felt deathly ill during the procedure. Being called back to the doctor's office to review a chest x-ray was highly unusual. Heading back to the clinic, I thought of all the possibilities I could be facing. My mind brought me back to my younger years when I must admit; I inhaled quite a few substances, one of which was tobacco.

Upon entering the examination room for the second time that day, I knew this would not be a pleasant meeting. My doctor pointed to my x-rays already up on his computer screen for viewing. There was a sizeable necrotic mass sitting in the upper lobe of my right lung. The radiologist interpreted this study as being "suspicious for pulmonary carcinoma."

After careful review and hoping against hope someone made a mistake, I turned back to my doctor as if to ask a question, but no words issued from my mouth. The expression on his face told me all I needed to know. Looking down and shaking his head from side to side, he said, in the most melancholy voice, "I am so very sorry, Sean."

Walking down the long corridor to exit the clinic, the only sounds I could hear were the pounding of my heart and the clip-clopping of my shoes on the ceramic floor beneath me. It seemed like every eye was focused directly on me as if to get one last look at this "dead man walking."

I recalled a time when I had the good fortune to work with a world-renowned cardiothoracic surgeon. While removing a cancerous lung from a middle-aged male, the doctor pointed to a spot on the patient's x-rays and said, "If you can see a mass any bigger than the size of a dime on a plain x-ray, the chances of that patient surviving for more than a year are slim." My lesion was the size of a walnut.

My greatest fear was not that I had developed lung cancer but for my family, especially my two teenage children, who would witness their father withering away in what is usually a cruel and painful death. The only thing I knew for sure was the need to get off this merry-go-round of negative thinking before returning home. I did not want to frighten my family unnecessarily before obtaining my CT scan results, and a lung biopsy scheduled over the next several days.

That day I refused to be admitted to the hospital as we were heading up north to hear our daughter, then president of her sorority, give an end-of-the-year presentation to her peers. When diagnosed with a disease like lung cancer, it is surprising how quickly one can slip into "This may be the last time I ever get the chance to do this" mode.

When life's proverbial shit hits the fan, I find great solace in spending some time alone at the beach. It is the contrast of the warm sun and the cool breeze, the feeling of the sand as it shifts beneath my feet, the salty mist of the surf as it fills my nostrils, and the sheer radiance of the ocean itself as if a thousand stars were dancing upon its surface that eases my troubled mind. The sea has always been "Dr. God's" homeopathic remedy to treat my wounded spirit.

I drove to an isolated beach in San Diego and sat on a large smooth rock that seemed to be handcrafted by the Almighty just for me. I closed my eyes and let mother nature do the rest. As my breathing became synchronized with the waves' rhythm, the physical tension and mental anxiety I had experienced earlier in the day began to dissipate. As I sank deeper into this meditative state, I heard that still, small voice within me asking, *why are you so afraid? Do you not remember?*

Now open to whatever divine guidance would have me to know, thoughts of my childhood raced through my mind. I sat motionless, watching this picture show of memories filter in and out of my consciousness. Some were joyful, others heart-wrenching. I sat there for quite some time until I was able to surrender to my new reality.

As I opened my eyes and became reacquainted with my surroundings, all my fears, including the fear of death itself, lost their power over me. I came to understand why I relied on chemicals to get me through life. But I also remembered the many hands of God who resurrected me from the bowels of hell, giving me another shot at life. I was confident that God, my family, and friends would once again help me defeat a most formidable foe.

Due to prudent fanatical planning, I knew my family would remain self-sufficient. My young and beautiful wife would meet someone new (of course not as chill as me) to share in her golden years. Most importantly, although I believed my children would like to have their dad around a little longer, they no longer needed my guidance. They were now mature enough and capable of handling all that life may throw their way, including the passing of their father.

# 2

# A HELL OF A TOWN

MANY WERE THE CHALLENGES NEW YORK CITY'S diverse ethnic groups had to face to earn their slice of the American pie. For those unfamiliar with the early history of New York and its role in welcoming our past generations into the land of the free, I would like to offer some tidbits from personal and historical perspectives.

When unveiled on October 28, 1896, a gift from the French, the Statue of Liberty stood at the mouth of New York harbor, pointing her beacon of light toward the heavens. She called out to all those who had ears to listen: "Give me your tired, your poor, your huddled masses yearning to breathe free." People longing for a better way of life from every corner of the earth heard this call to freedom. Waves of immigrants risked their very lives to reach the shores of these United States.

From 1892 until her doors closed permanently in 1954, Ellis Island was the most active immigrant processing center in America.

More than twelve million immigrants worldwide passed through her gates. In its first year of operation, Ellis Island welcomed close to half a million immigrants to the "land of opportunity."

In the 1840s and '50s, immigrants from Germany and Ireland, and later from Italy and China, forever changed New York City's landscape. These fledgling citizens of the United States settled into distinct ethnic neighborhoods. They worked hard, raised families, and turned many of their native customs and culinary specialties into successful businesses. The city was coming of age.

To realize the American dream, new immigrants had little choice but to join unions and political organizations usually associated with their ethnic origins. These groups used their sheer member numbers to convince local candidates to support additional services in their districts and provide greater access to good-paying jobs. This practice of quid pro quo continues today in American politics, but in a more tech-savvy way.

A film I never tire of watching, West Side Story won ten Academy Awards in 1962, including the Oscar for best picture. In the movie, Maria portrayed brilliantly by actress Natalie Wood, and her Puerto Rican friends sing, "I like to be in America. Okay, by me in America. Everything's free in America; I want to be in America." The song was upbeat and hopeful but so far from the truth. Everything was possible, but nothing was free in America.

In the mid-to-late 1800s, freed slaves comprised most of the labor workforce in New York City. If the German and Irish immigrants wanted to find work and move up the ranks, they needed to work harder, extended hours, and receive less pay than those who came before them. Likewise, the Italians and Chinese who arrived later were required to do the same. Most new arrivals settled in lower Manhattan, where the best opportunities were for finding work.

With all its hopes and promises, New York City could also be an island of quicksand for those immigrants who could not or refused to comply with her rules. And yes, there have always been rules. These "codes of conduct" were dictated by whatever ethnic group was the most prominent, politically connected, and ruthless at the time.

The Italians just so happened to be "the dog that bit the hand" of the Irish. Although the Italians arrived decades after the Irish, they quickly became the most dominant force throughout New York City and remain so today. We would all be wise to remember, however, that every dog has its day!

Our early city planners could not comprehend the magnitude of growth that New York City was about to experience. New York's architects believed the city would not expand any further north than nineteen blocks. Today, from north to south, approximately 382 blocks comprise Manhattan.

In 1895, the residents of Queens, Brooklyn, Staten Island, and the Bronx, all independent cities, voted to consolidate with Manhattan to become the five boroughs of the Greater New York Area. In 1904, New York City's transit system began operating and became the catalyst that made New York the melting pot it is today. Those who worked in Manhattan could now live in any other borough where housing was more affordable.

Throughout its early evolution, corruption in politics and within the ranks of union leaders ran rampant. Political organizations like Irish Tammany Hall, which formed in 1789, exercised tremendous power due to its ability to guarantee political candidates large voter turnouts. Although synonymous with corruption, Tammany Hall remained politically untouchable and endured for nearly two centuries.

During Mayor LaGuardia's leadership (1934–45), the city flourished at an accelerated rate. Many distinct neighborhoods, such as the Financial District, Chelsea, the Fashion District, Soho, Broadway, the Diamond District, Little Italy, Chinatown, Alphabet City, Hell's Kitchen, and Spanish Harlem began to take shape. These neighborhoods all had their share of local hoodlums, petty thieves, and drug pushers, but five Italian families dominated organized crime.

A small section of town, expanding from West 34th to 59th streets, known as Hell's Kitchen, remained out of the Italian mob's reach. Former mayor Rudy Giuliani referred to the Westies as "The most ruthless gang in the history of organized crime." This close-knit group of young Irishmen was fearless, tenacious, and well-disciplined. The Westies excelled in drug distribution, extortion, loan sharking, as well as murder for hire.

The Westies, known for killing their rivals and spreading their body parts throughout the city, sent a clear message to everyone, including the five families who might challenge their dominance in the area.

I loved the stories my mother told about growing up in Hell's Kitchen. It was in this neighborhood where I developed the only real connection I ever felt with my Irish heritage.

By now, you may have concluded this author is biased in my perspectives of New York, offering only a dim, distorted, one-sided view of the city that never sleeps. Nothing can be further from the truth. I have a profound love and deep respect for my birthplace and for the many opportunities it had to offer. As I decided not to write this book in novel form, I feel somewhat obligated to share the truth as I know the truth to be. My fellow New Yorkers would put it this way: "If it is what it is, it was what it was."

# 3

# THE KINGS OF QUEENS

I GREW UP IN A SMALL BUT INTEGRAL PART OF THE borough of Queens. Generations ago, William Steinway, the founder of the Steinway Piano Company, purchased some four hundred acres of land in our developing neighborhood. Their main factory stood out like a sore thumb among the various construction sites, bocce-ball courts, and live-kill butcheries.

This company's impact on our neighborhood's development was transformational—other companies followed by moving their operations from Manhattan to Queens, creating good-paying jobs for local workers. The Steinways donated vast amounts of money and land to the community, built a church, post office, firehouse, library, and a public school that was one of the country's first free kindergartens.

Only blocks away, you could smell way before you could see our local garbage dump. "The dumps," as referred to by our neighborhood's elite, was one of my favorite places to sling marbles at rats as they dodged in and out of the rocks and debris. If you needed to take a dump yourself, you could do so here with impunity. Finding a few fresh leaves ahead of time was not mandatory, but it could be quite beneficial in the end.

At Queensboro Plaza, the R train, which originates at Ditmars Boulevard in Astoria, connects with other trains arriving from Woodside, Jackson Heights, Elmhurst, Flushing, and Long Island City. As the train enters the plaza, it screeches and grinds around a steep curve, tilting some twenty degrees to the right, five stories above ground level. At times like these, the elderly ladies dressed in black clutched their rosary beads and began to pray.

When the inevitable long delays occurred, one could amuse themselves by looking down from the elevated tracks to the unrelenting traffic morass below. Commuters from all parts of Queens and Long Island jockeyed for position to maneuver their way over the Queensboro (aka 59th Street) Bridge into Manhattan.

The real challenge for my fellow New Yorkers below the plaza was not in their infamous driving skills but their proficiency in the fine art of horn honking. One must be faster, louder, and more annoying than anyone else to make it over the bridge and get to work on time.

Like me, if you have a morbid fascination with death, you could also gaze across the plaza to stare into the windows of the Brothers in Arms Casket Company. Your imagination could run wild, filling each shiny mahogany box with people you wished were no longer part of your inner circle.

After packing its cars with early morning zombies sipping their morning coffee, the R train proceeds through the East River tunnel into Manhattan. This tunnel, built on the bottom of the river, was the last obstacle the train faced before exiting on Fifty-Ninth Street and Lexington Avenue. Back then, there was not an automobile assembled anywhere on earth that could survive such a journey.

Predictably, as the train begins its voyage through the tunnel, the lights inside the passenger cars darkened, causing its riders to become acutely aware of their surroundings. The male perverts would have already positioned themselves near an attractive woman or a cute little boy waiting for the train to rock violently, so they could "accidentally" bump into their favorite private parts. Please do not ask how I knew all that. As one could no longer view their favorite pornographic magazine hidden within their newspaper, they may try napping. However, they did so only if they were no longer interested in keeping the golden crucifix they wore around their neck.

If one chooses to keep their eyes open, they may quickly realize the terrible mistake they just made. As the train travels through the tunnel, it passes a few strategically placed sixty-watt bulbs hanging from a single wire, illuminating water dripping from the walls and ceiling. Claustrophobics were required to triple their medication intake before embarking on such a journey.

Looking east toward LaGuardia Airport was, without a doubt, the most annoying "white bread" section of town, displaying row after row of single-family homes with paved driveways, manicured lawns, and various fruit trees ripe for the picking. On the corners in this neighborhood, you might find an occasional mom-and-pop grocery store or a bakery, but not one gang of kids hanging out—my God, what a waste of a perfectly good corner.

If you were heading west, you would be on a collision course with our government-subsidized housing units. Our code of conduct mandated that whites did not come within a block of the projects, and blacks and Puerto Ricans were not to cross the east side of 31st Street. If everyone respected these ethnic boundaries, our neighborhood remained relatively peaceful.

The East River, infamously known for holding the record for the highest number of "floaters" (including separate body parts) in a single year, divides our western border from the east side of Manhattan. Stretching south for almost a mile was a popular community park, an oasis from the city's everyday hustle and bustle.

If you could find one, you could sit on a patch of grass amid broken glass and dried-up condoms, watching the mighty tugboats navigate block-long barges through the treacherous waters of the East River. From this vantage point, you could look on as the never-ending stream of automobiles and trucks bounce from one pothole to another along the East River Drive.

The Parkside Gents, one of the first nationally recognized gangs in the United States, also called Queens their home. In my opinion, this "gang" was nothing more than a leftover doo-wop band from the 1950s. You could usually find its members lurking in the shadows of storefronts and alleyways throughout the neighborhood, sniffing glue and drinking codeine-based cough syrup. They wore black leather jackets, Levi's, and Converse sneakers. They sang songs from The Drifters, The Platters, Smokey Robinson, and of course, the king of rock & roll, Elvis Presley. Toward the southern end of the park was a community pool that anyone with two bits in their pockets or the ability to hop a fence could get in.

High above and cutting through the park's center, the Hell Gate Bridge stood barely used and neglected for many years. When completed in 1916, the Hell Gate was the longest steel arch bridge in the world. During World War II, this bridge was targeted for destruction by Nazis, but agents from the United States thwarted the plot.

As teenagers, in an unintentional attempt to find God, we learned how to pray by climbing the Hell Gate's massive granite base some four stories above ground level. While sitting on the top platform, an unexpected gust of wind or a few cold beers could lead to a meeting with your Maker much earlier than your parents anticipated.

Our apartment complex, known by us simple folks as the Mets, was a group of five-story walk-up brick buildings. The Mets held the distinct honor of housing my clan for more than two decades. Its compound encompassed two square blocks in the center of town.

Each block consisted of seven buildings, mirror images of themselves facing back-to-back. In the center, separating the two rows of buildings was what management called our garden area. Within the garden area were only a dozen or so living trees and bushes with a handful of planted flowers that did not have a chance in hell of surviving more than a week. Its soil was so hard we routinely cracked our helmets on it while playing football in the winter.

Separating each of the buildings were alleyways, where tenants were required to place our trash inside one of the dozens of large aluminum cans provided. Our superintendents routinely instructed us about securing the lids on the containers so the cats and rats could not feast on the rubbish. My friends and I were a little more creative than those in management, as we found more exciting ways to utilize these lids. In the summer, they became our shields, protecting us from the onslaught of broomsticks, baseball bats, tree branches, and car antennas that swung in our direction as we played Gladiator, one of my favorite summer sports.

In the winter, these shields helped protect the forts we constructed from discarded Christmas trees and packed snow, sheltering us from enemy snowball attacks that occurred several times a day without warning. We later torched these trees in a spectacular display of recklessness during our Annual New Year's Eve Garden Area Bonfire.

My favorite way of utilizing these lids was on July 4th, when we magically transformed them into flying saucers by igniting M-80s underneath them in the middle of the street. We believed if NASA could send rockets into space, we had the God-given right to launch our saucers a few hundred feet into the air. However, the principle of gravity dictates, "What goes up must come down," and unfortunately for some, our flying saucers had a mind of their own.

Each building had basements accessible through doors in every alleyway. These tunnels of love were a dream come true for any horny, prepubescent young man looking for his first conquest. If I were with a young lady who wanted to "ball," I would check every door in the complex until I found one that was unlocked or figured out a way to jimmy it open. One of the spiritual teachings I remembered growing up was, "When one door closes, another door opens." This lesson was indeed very "good news" to me.

Our building code required we have fire escapes accessible from both the roof and ground level. Anyone could access the system in an alleyway, climb up to the roof, and descend one of the four staircases leading into the courtyard. Having this ability gave us access to enter our apartments (or any other) through the kitchen windows, all facing the courtyard below, making the need for carrying keys almost obsolete.

Our garden area also served as our backup alley for those tenants who were not capable of or unwilling to walk down the stairs to dump their trash. They would open their window, pretend to be talking to someone across the way, drop their unwanted items, then quickly disappeared back inside their apartment. This method—The Houdini—was preferred mostly by those tenants living on the upper floors.

My family lived in a fifth-floor corner apartment that provided a panoramic view of all the action happening in the streets below. On the downside, it was on the top floor of a five-story walkup. And just for the record, I am not copping to throwing any trash out of our apartment windows. Our apartment consisted of three bedrooms, two, 8x10, the typical size of a jail cell on Riker's Island. We had a small living room, a tiny dining room, and a minuscule kitchen. There was only one bathroom for all seven of us who lived there.

In our neighborhood, most women were content in their traditional roles as wives, mothers, and homemakers. Our fathers were mostly middle-class, blue-collar workers. Our dads became police officers, firefighters, sanitation workers, plumbers, carpenters, dockworkers, shop owners, and a handful of petty thieves.

Most families were Roman Catholics who attended church "religiously" on most Sundays, Easter, and Christmas. Does this not sound like the only thing we needed to make an urban style Ozzie and Harriet's movie was a Pit Bull named Lassie? Most of our families may have fit into that all-American family stereotype, but not the seven of us, dancing with the devil in our cockroach-infested fifth-floor apartment.

Ours would have been your stereotypical Irish-American

neighborhood, but for one thing only, the Italians. The Italian mobsters dominated the rackets in every part of our community. Real gangsters were easy to identify as they operated out in the open without concern for the police. These were the men who drove fancy cars and wore sharkskin suits, fedora hats, and green alligator shoes.

Queens did not have the burned-out and abandoned buildings easily found in Harlem, Bedford-Stuyvesant, and throughout the Bronx, but we did have our share of burned-out people. There were many Irish gangster wannabes in our neighborhood, but I cannot think of one who commanded the same level of respect as the Italians. So, along with my ever-maturing and socially acceptable prejudices against blacks, Puerto Ricans, and Jews, I began to develop my most deep-rooted hatred toward the Irish, of which I was one.

# 4

# BORN UNDER A SAD SIGN

Y PARENTS WERE BORN AT A PIVOTAL TIME IN OUR nation's history. Their generation is called "the greatest generation" for good reasons. These Americans not only lived through the Great Depression but a World War that killed more than sixty million people, 3 percent of the entire population of the planet. This madness was primarily due to the actions taken by one of the most depraved psychopaths the world has ever known, Adolf Hitler.

My father, a first-generation Irish American born in 1917, was one of nine children whose parents emigrated from County Cork, Ireland, and settled in Brooklyn. During the Second World War, my dad served in the US Army but remained stateside. His records indicate he required emergency surgery for a bleeding gastric ulcer. Eventually, he received a medical discharge due to his "nerves."

My mother was born in 1918, two years before women fought for and won the right to vote, was the oldest of three children born to first-generation German immigrants. Her older sister died in her early forties due to complications from acute lymphocytic leukemia. She left behind a sweet, kind, and loving daughter in her early twenties to take care of her physically challenged, schizophrenic father until his passing many years later.

Her brother served in the Pacific Theater during the Second World War in an army unit credited with liberating parts of the Philippine Islands. He called receiving the "Philippine Medal of Freedom" his proudest moment. The one request he had for when he died was to have this medal pinned to his chest when buried. Thirty years after the war ended, my uncle also played a vital role in our family's deliverance.

Although my mother claimed to be German-Irish, we have never found anything linking back to her Irish heritage. Her grandmother, Hannah Lutz, emigrated from Eastern Europe and settled in what is now known as Hell's Kitchen. Records from Ellis Island indicate that Hannah was of Jewish descent, making this Irish-German Italian wannabe a Jew.

I always thought my mother claimed to be half Irish due to her connections in Hell's Kitchen and to appease her pathologically proud Irish in-laws. However, recently, one of my sisters had her DNA tested, which revealed no Eastern European genealogy in our family's ancestry. Go figure!

The story told is that my parents met in the romantic setting of an art class in Hell's Kitchen. If true, they must have abandoned their passion for the arts in the years that followed. The first time I ever saw my mother paint was after her seventy-eighth birthday when she received a Bob Ross professional art kit from one of my sisters.

Although my father had distinctive and beautifully crafted handwriting, I never saw him participate in anything artistic. Later in life, my dad's writing remained distinct but looked like he was using a vibrator to write instead of a pen.

My parents married before the defeat of Nazi Germany and the surrender of Japan in 1945. They had their first child in March of 1944. Four more children followed. It appeared the best time for baby-making activities was in the winter of 1953, as the "personality kid," as nicknamed by my mother, was born the following fall. By all accounts, life was simpler back then, but not necessarily easier.

There were no personal computers, as Al Gore had not yet invented the internet. Cell phones were about the size of a loaf of bread and rarely seen. If one needed to communicate by telephone, they most likely used a standard, all-black AT&T rotary phone, which required you to dial all seven to ten numbers yourself. Could you imagine such a thing? Facebook, texting, email, and tweeting were not yet words added to Webster's Dictionary.

Television shows like *Leave it to Beaver, The Honeymooners, Fathers Knows Best,* and *The Brady Bunch* led in the ratings. Most TV families, including cartoons like *The Flintstones* and *The Jetsons,* had one thing in common: two very loving and, of course, white parents, one male, one female, living in the home. These parents rarely argued, at least not in front of the children. If they ever disagreed, they settled their differences before the end of each episode.

The most controversial sitcom on TV in the 1970s was *All in the Family,* featuring the incorrigible Archie Bunker, played by veteran actor Carroll O'Connor. It would almost be impossible for Archie to function in our society today, for politically correct he was not. At least to me, this family appeared more realistic than all the others. Besides, I loved that Archie, Edith, Gloria, and Mike, the "Meathead," all lived in Queens.

If looking down from our fifth-floor apartment, Norman Rockwell might be inclined to paint a scene depicting the milkman, iceman, and paperboy making their early morning deliveries. Some tenants helped in the delivery process by lowering wicker baskets from their windows to retrieve the items. The always crafty drug dealers picked up on this idea and began using fishing poles from the hallway windows to complete their transactions. With spotters on the roof and numerous ways to escape, it made it nearly impossible to get busted.

Rockwell's painting might also depict Dr. Kramer, our

neighborhood physician, on his way to another house call. With him would be a little black bag full of reusable needles and syringes, along with penicillin, dispensed liberally for five bucks a pop. John, the florist, always behind schedule, creating another over-the-top floral arrangement destined for one of the guests in a local funeral home. And Giovanni, the shoemaker, who spoke no English, working diligently to repair the many shoes left in his shop.

Let us not forget Father Saraceno, walking solemnly to deliver the last rites of the Church to a dying (most likely already dead) parishioner. Highlighted in the painting would be the excitement and sheer terror on the children's faces as they sat on the Half Moon, a traveling carnival ride. The operator would manually swing the moon up and down as the little ones screamed in unison, "Higher, higher, higher."

On the international front, the United States was losing the Vietnam war, both overseas and in the ever-growing collective consciousness of its citizens. Most Americans were now solidly against this police action that killed more than fifty-eight thousand American soldiers and countless North and South Vietnamese men, women, and children. There was a new revolution taking place in the streets of America.

As our soldiers fought to free Southeast Asia from the communist threat, citizens in this country were still fighting for their fundamental civil rights. On May 4, 1970, members of the Ohio National Guard shot and killed four unarmed students at Kent State University, exercising their constitutional right to free speech. They were demanding an end to this senseless war. I believe this incident at Kent State turned the tide in this country against the war in Vietnam.

The Cold War with the Soviet Union reached a boiling point. Pro-communist Cuban dictator Fidel Castro invited the Soviets to install several nuclear missile sites in Cuba, just ninety miles off the Florida coast. The impossible was now possible—mutually assured destruction. Its acronym MAD was most appropriate. Our clueless leaders in Washington advised school-age children throughout the states to hide under our desks if attacked by a thermonuclear device.

In the 1960s, President John F. Kennedy, his brother, Bobby Kennedy, and Martin Luther King Jr. were all assassinated by gunfire. On November 17, 1973, in one of the most humiliating events in American political history, Richard M. Nixon stood in front of the international press and proclaimed to the world, "I am not a crook."

History has proven Nixon was a crook. He resigned from the office of the presidency rather than face the certainty of impeachment proceedings. Soon after his resignation, "Tricky Dick" received a full pardon for his involvement in the coverup of the Watergate Hotel break-in by his former vice president and now president of the United States, Gerald R. Ford. A simpler life? Like my ass!

# 5

# BIG O, LITTLE o, UH-OH

A S SOON AS I PUT MY INITIAL THOUGHTS FOR THIS
book on paper, my typical egocentric debate began raging
between my ears. *Are you out of your freaking mind? What makes
you think an idiot like you would be capable of writing such a book?
Remember, you're the one who got left-back in the second and sixth
grades. You're computer illiterate. You still type with two fingers, and
you're going to do what? Don't be stupid, stupid.*

According to Wikipedia, imposter syndrome (a term coined in
1978 by clinical psychologists Dr. Pauline Clance and Suzanne Imes)
is "a concept describing high-achieving individuals marked by an
inability to internalize their accomplishments and a persistent fear of
being exposed as a fraud." This mind-set was prevalent throughout
my entire career in orthopedics.

My deep-seated feelings of inadequacy showed up with guns
blazing while attending social events with highly intelligent and
successful people. I always felt like an outsider looking in, as if

watching my life unfold on a movie screen. This merry-go-round of gobbledygook keeps addicts frozen in time, rendering us powerless to fulfill the dreams we hold for ourselves and others.

When asked, most of my friends say they can remember as far back as when they were three or four years old. My earliest memory does not occur until I was about nine. My younger brother, "Pookey," was in the living room wearing only a pair of dirty white briefs performing his legionary "freak dance." His skinny, almost emaciated body looked as if he was experiencing a grand mal seizure. As a side note, I once dated a girl that referred to her private parts as Pookey. Am I missing something here?

I am aware of some experiences I had earlier than nine. However, this awareness comes not from memory alone but from the many photographs and countless stories told and retold by family members over the years. I know I attended kindergarten at a private Catholic school. I also know I once wore a bright red with yellow polka dot shirt for picture day in the fourth grade. I did not need the red nose and a colorful wig to feel like a clown that day. And at six years old, when stricken with a severe case of measles, I was photographed snatching a box of cherry Jell-O from the bottom shelf of the kitchen cabinet.

This lapse of memory may have been unfortunate for my writings here today but may have been the very mechanism I needed back then to survive. Over the years, I have come to believe the human spirit can tolerate only a limited amount of emotional trauma before it shuts down completely.

When one reaches their maximum capacity for emotional pain, they will build thick, impenetrable walls to prevent any further insult to their mental well-being. I guess I should be grateful for my early absence of memory, for my real-life nightmare was about to begin.

One evening I watched an exposé on television spotlighting a bizarre psychological condition known as multiple personality disorder. The audience got introduced to an otherwise unremarkable, healthy-looking man in his mid-thirties who suffered from MPD.

This bruised, battered, and tattered young man developed eight distinct and easily accessible personalities during his childhood. These included a flamboyant gay attention seeker, a disconnected older brother, and an aggressive, impulsive, and undisciplined alpha male.

As a child, this boy's mother called him stupid, evil, and worthless. To teach him how to behave like all the other boys, she locked him in his bedroom closet with little to eat or drink for days at a time. His clothing soiled with excrement. During the interview, he related that his greatest fears came to life while imprisoned in the closet. As the sun closed its weary eyes, the closet became a playground for a family of mice that never seemed to run out of energy.

This segment also included an interview with an internationally renowned psychiatrist, recognized for developing effective treatments for this disorder. The doctor explained that patients afflicted with MPD create various personas to distribute the amount of their emotional pain with "the others." By doing so, they no longer needed to absorb the totality of these horrendous experiences by themselves.

Watching this story unfold, I experienced a profound sense of empathy, not only for this troubled young man but for a thin, freckled-faced little boy who once took a school picture wearing a red with yellow polka dots shirt. People recently have become interested in developing better memory skills by taking an abundance of vitamin supplements and jumping on the Luminosity bandwagon. However, it may be necessary for some of us to cultivate what my late friend and Unity Minister, Eric Butterworth referred to as "a good forgettery."

One evening, my wife and I went out to eat in a local Indian community where the smell of curry permeated the night air. Surrounded by the many restaurants and shops sits a modest Hindu temple. That evening, Diwali, "The Festival of Lights," was being celebrated. Worshipers came dressed in their traditional attire, celebrating inside and outside the temple. Most sang and danced in the streets, while the more devoted continued to pray inside the temple. Around the entrance door stood a three-foot-high pile of shoes left respectfully behind by those entering. I paused for a moment to reflect on a story I heard many years ago about a man who complained about not having shoes until he met a man who had no feet.

I wondered what the worshipers might do when leaving the temple if they had the opportunity to pick any pair of shoes out of the pile and claim them as their own. However, by doing so, they must assume the original owner's complete identity, their age, health, condition of their finances, the love or lack of love they feel, and all the memories of their past experiences.

Many of us raised in this self-absorbed, "poor me" society tend to believe the grass is always greener on the other side. We view the cup as half empty instead of half full. And instead of being grateful for what we have, we focus on the few things we do not have. Given the same opportunity, most of us would take the same shoes we walked in with back out of the pile. Some tend to experience high levels of anxiety when stepping into anything new.

I am sure my family's story is not much different from the millions of other families who have experienced addiction in their homes. Its far-reaching tentacles will prey upon and methodically squeeze the life out of everyone living under its rule. As a child, it seemed my father's side of the family was not quite like that of my mother's. My father's side of the family was unlike any other family I have ever known.

Whenever we traveled to Brooklyn to visit my paternal grandparents, everyone in the house was bitter, boisterous, and blurry-eyed. A thick plume of smoke hovered just below the ceiling. Although one would be hard-pressed to find a container of milk or juice in the refrigerator, there was never a shortage of bourbon and beer. The conversation at the dinner table inevitably revolved around how the government, their bosses, neighbors, and especially the blacks were screwing them over, preventing them from getting ahead in life.

My mother became the glue that held our family together. If it were not for her unwavering encouragement, this story would have a much different ending. She was our sergeant-at-arms, a vigilant soldier protecting us from a prolific assassin that invaded our home. My mom had an uncanny ability to accept life's many challenges in stride. My father, not so much. Come rain or shine; my dad lived on the edge.

Although my father had an arsenal of profanities at his disposal, his all-time favorite was, "Jesus, Mary, and Joseph, have mercy on me." When he invoked both Jesus and His parents, we all knew it was time to run for the hills. During these outbreaks, my dad gritted his teeth so tightly I believed his brains would eventually pop out of his head.

An uncontrollable temper was not my father's only shortcoming. He was a functioning alcoholic who smoked two packs of unfiltered cigarettes a day and was a compulsive gambler. No horse was running on any track in the country that my dad would not risk betting everything he had. After watching his paycheck gallop away, he needed to borrow money from our neighbors, coworkers, or the local bookie to cover the bills.

Like most addicts, against all evidence to the contrary, my father was convinced his luck was about to change. He would promise, "The next time, things will be different." My father's biggest challenge was to convince those he already owed money to that he was about to hit it big. But things were never different; our luck never changed.

Due to the usual and customary nonpayment of our gas, electric, and telephone bills, these services were routinely "Discontinued until further notice." At times, not having electricity and having to light candles around the apartment could be fun. However, it was never fun trying to sleep during the winter in a virtual icebox with only the darkness and my thoughts in hand.

Mother, who was creative in the kitchen, always came up with something to put on the table. Her go-to meal was hot milk with steamed rice, sprinkled with sugar and cinnamon. At times this was our breakfast, lunch, and dinner for days at a time. Monotonous, you say? Maybe, but it filled our bellies. Any hot meal was much appreciated, especially on those harsh New York winter nights.

During a family reunion in Cancun, Mexico, all my siblings agreed that the one aspect of our father's addiction we feared most was his unpredictability. You never knew how he was going to react in any given situation. The day I brought home my sixth-grade report card indicating I needed to repeat the year, I thought it would be the last day of my life. Instead of the ass-whooping I was expecting, my dad sat me on his lap, drunk and drooling, telling me what a great kid I was.

We recalled a time when we were all sitting around the dining room table, feasting on a hot pot of spaghetti and meatballs. We could always rely on my father to arrive home late from work after having a nightcap or two at a neighborhood bar. This night would not be any different. After stumbling through the doorway, he sat in his customary place at the head of the table. My mom got up and served him a generous plate of hot food.

After sitting for a few minutes, he stood up and, without saying a word, threw his entire plate of spaghetti against the dining room wall. My mother intercepted him on his way to their bedroom, chastising him about his irresponsibility to the family. Not willing to listen to any of my mom's criticism, he pushed her aside and went to bed. Uh-oh!

I never saw my mother get that angry before or since. She paced back and forth like a lioness in a cage, mumbling the words she would soon be reciting to her unsuspecting, semiconscious prey. When my dad began snoring, she grabbed a broomstick from the kitchen and marched into their bedroom. Within seconds, we heard the first swoosh as she brought it down to bear on my father's shins.

The following morning, my father was slower than usual, getting out of bed. Instead of his typical early morning leave-me-alone face, fear was the face du jour.

My mom walked straight up to him, eyeball to eyeball, and said, "If you ever touch me again, you son of a bitch, it will not be a broomstick but a butcher knife I will bring into the bedroom." I think my dad got the point.

My mother told us years later that this was the first and last time my father ever laid a hand on her. They divorced within a year, but that was one hell of a year. Every evening before heading off to bed, we barricaded our apartment door with furniture. We also booby-trapped our kitchen window with razor blades and wire so unwelcomed guests could not make their way inside unannounced.

After the divorce, my dad disappeared for a while, eventually setting up his new digs in northern Virginia. I got to see him one last time before he left the city. As I was boarding a bus in Queens, my dad was standing in the back facing me. When our eyes met, he appeared more anxious than I. At the next stop, he got off the bus, not saying a word to me, pretending he never saw me in the first place. This encounter remains one of my most painful childhood memories.

# 6

# INTO THE LIONS DEN

IN FUTURE CHAPTERS, I WILL BE DISCUSSING THE SIGNS, symptoms, and all the naughty nuances of this always underestimated and often fatal disease. Due to the resurgence of heroin and prescription opiate consumption in small-town America, addiction is once again reaching the level of attention it deserves.

If you haven't noticed, addiction is no longer just an inner-city problem. This menace has established deep-seated roots in rural communities throughout this great land. If we ever hope to slow down our national body bag count, we must first change our pie in the sky attitude toward addiction.

At this juncture, I believe it is essential for the reader to have at least a basic understanding of what I refer to as the "true nature of addiction." Ask yourself this. When introduced to a stimulus we somehow find comforting, why do some of us continue to do it habitually to great peril, while most of us would not give it a second thought?

With a shout-out to my fellow procrastinators, let's take a quick time out here. I would like you to write a list of all the things you know in your heart of hearts that are not in your best interest but keep repeating them anyway. To some, it may come as a surprise that using drugs, drinking alcohol, overeating, or smoking cigarettes may identify some of the manifestations of addiction but do not define addiction itself.

I have read articles espousing scientific evidence of a genetic link to addiction. I do not dispute this evidence. However, I do not believe it is the predominant cause of why people develop chemical dependencies. I think it is the psychosocial atmosphere of those susceptible to addiction find themselves in without acquiring the necessary coping skills to adapt. Once again, our children are the most vulnerable among us.

Addicts never choose to be so. If we were to ask a five-year-old what she wants to be when she grows up, she would most likely reply, "I want to be a doctor, an attorney, a nurse, a teacher, an entertainer, or a professional athlete." You will never hear a child say, "I want to become an alcoholic like my father and die from cirrhosis of the liver."

Children never say, "I want to smoke methamphetamine like my mother, so my teeth will disintegrate in my mouth." Or think, *After college, I want to shoot heroin and cocaine so I can choose to die from an overdose, hepatitis, AIDS, or in the streets by the hands of another.* Most of us who become addicted will spend a significant portion of our lives trying to recover from this dreadful "dis-ease."

Addiction is a complex, multifaceted disease that affects a person physically, mentally, and spiritually. I believe the underlying cause of addiction is a spiritual deficiency, an emptiness of the spirit that drives those addicted to numb their emotional pain no matter what the cost. You may assume since my father was out of the picture long before I ever picked up my first drug, I may have escaped such a fate. Your assumption, however, would be incorrect.

If we ever hope to help those suffering from this hideous

disease, we must first come to grips that addiction is not a chemical process. It is a deep, dark, never-ending emptiness of the human spirit. Unfortunately, my father grew up in the same psychosocial atmosphere that all his children and some of his grandchildren must now endure.

My dad unwittingly placed all five of his children on death row, waiting for the executioner to show up and hand out the poison. My brothers and sisters all believe our father loved us but could never admit his powerlessness over his addiction. My poor father never gave himself a chance to recover. He was cremated with all his insanity still intact.

Speaking in my native tongue, back in "doze days," all my teachers, fellow students, and everyone in my neighborhood knew my parents divorced. Having families separating in the 1960s was an oddity. Most of the conversations I had back then usually started with a pat on my back, followed by the same two well-meaning questions: Are you guys doing okay? Do you know where your dad is? His bookies added, Do you know if he is ever coming back?

As a kid, I learned to be a chameleon, always conscious of projecting the family's illusion of normalcy out in the community. In the seventh grade, Mother Superior, the top nun in charge, summoned me to her office. My teachers reported that I hung around the schoolyard on most days during our lunch break instead of going home to eat.

Mother Superior was concerned I was not getting enough nourishment during the day to function well enough in the classroom. She believed hunger might be a contributing factor to my clear and present apathy toward my schoolwork. The first lesson we learn when enrolling in Addiction 101 is not to talk about the family's business outside of the family. In our family, that was easy; we never discussed family business, even within the family. The day my father splattered his plate of spaghetti against the wall, the rest of us finished our meal without anyone saying a word about what just happened.

Mother Superior and I sat on opposite ends of her desk. She

stared at me in silence with that "I gotcha" look on her face. So I did what I learned to do so well over the years; I made up a story.

I looked up and spoke to her as if I genuinely believed what I was saying. I told her she had it all wrong; we had plenty of food at home. In fact, on that very day, I had two hamburgers and a tall glass of milk for lunch. I perfected this deception of normalcy not only with those in authority but with my friends, classmates, and neighbors.

After my parents' divorce, my oldest sister married an economics professor and moved to Canada to raise a family. My older brother joined the navy and spent most of his time on an aircraft carrier positioned off the coast of Southeast Asia. The younger of my two sisters attended nursing school, and soon after graduation, she married her childhood sweetheart and moved to the suburbs. It was now up to me, the man of the house, to defend our little castle in the sky.

I learned how to become the adopted son of my friends' parents, often landing me a hot meal plus a doggie bag to bring home for my brother. I believe these families enjoyed having me over as I was always good for a laugh. I not only became the class clown but the family and neighborhood clown as well. Let me tell you; Bozo had nothing on me.

I am going to share with you two truths and a lie. Your job will be to guess which one is untrue. (1) I never smoked crack cocaine or methamphetamine; (2) I received a formal exorcism by a Bishop in the Roman Catholic Church; (3) I am a second-degree black belt in Tae Kwon Do. The answer lies behind door number three. I am a third-degree black belt. So, sit with that for a few minutes. Now ask yourself, *Am I sure I want to read the rest of this book?*

If my thesis is correct, and the predominant cause of addiction is a spiritual void, organized religion was the hand that hammered the final nails into my coffin. As you read this chapter, I ask you to please understand, it is not my intention, nor my style, to misrepresent the church or its educational system in any way, shape, or form. I am sharing my experiences only and do not speak for anyone but myself.

Over the millennium, religious-based organizations have helped millions of people throughout the world. These are my personal experiences that occurred four to five decades ago. My intention here is to give the reader an insight into how a child's already low self-esteem can progress to a point where that child loses all sense of self-worth.

When I attended grade school, corporal punishment was not only permitted but encouraged by our parents. If I ever told my parents a teacher struck me, I would undoubtedly get punished a second time. Once again, the lesson for me was to keep my mouth shut.

I am happy to report that as an altar boy, I was not one of the many molested by priests. However, I was propositioned by one in my early thirties while attending an adult Bible study class. This time I did not keep my mouth shut. And please, do not read anything into that.

If a teacher needed to make an example out of anyone, I would be the first to admit I gave my teachers plenty of ammunition to make me their primary target. When you become the class clown, your classmates may find you funny, but those in authority will resent you. I tried every trick in the book not to go to school, including making up diseases our scientists had not yet discovered.

Even when I made it to class, consciously, I was never there. If I were attending grammar school today, the teachers would insist I take ADHD medication. While at school, my favorite pastimes were making out with girls in the cloakroom and sitting at my desk watching the clock as it ticked ever so slowly toward my daily liberation.

For most students, Fridays were the happiest day of the week, but not for me. On Fridays, our school held its weekly detention. Detention was for those students caught talking in line or walking out of formation. It consisted of sitting in a classroom with your hands folded without speaking, fifteen minutes for each infraction.

Two was the average amount of tickets we troublemakers would usually accumulate in any given week.

Every Friday, a student was selected to announce the names of those who were to report to the detention area after the three o'clock bell rang. They picked me to make the announcements on a day I wished I were not so honored. I was to read the students' names in alphabetical order and state how many tickets they received.

When I got to the letter H, I started giggling and then belly-laughed into the microphone. "Sean Harrison, room 202, twelve tickets." Twelve was not only a class record but a new school record as well.

I knew my amusement over this situation was going to be short-lived. During these detention periods, Father Anderson, the chief of police (sorry, I meant to say the chief priest), made a cameo appearance to dish out corporal punishment to all of us evildoers for the redemption of our sins.

It appeared Father Anderson did not share the same celebratory attitude for my record-breaking abilities as I did. Most students had a choice of getting smacked over their knuckles with a wooden ruler or bent over and whacked on the butt with a three-quarter inch paddle. Father Anderson gave me no such opportunity.

As he called each student up to the front of the classroom to receive their just due, he skipped over my name and left me for last. To me, this indicated one of two possibilities. Either he was going to let me go scot-free, or I was in deep trouble. Would anyone care to venture a guess as to what happened next?

By the time it was all said and done, the knuckles on both my hands were bleeding, and as I slid back into my desk, I must have resembled the Leaning Tower of Pisa, tilting some thirty degrees to the right.

Fridays were also the day of the week when we students marched two by two from our classrooms into the church next door for mandatory confessions. I believe even the likes of Mother Teresa would feel intimidated by this process. The confessionals looked like three six-foot-tall mahogany coffins standing upright, joined-together by shiny brass trim depicting an assortment of religious symbols.

My personal favorite, of course, was the evil slithery serpent. I believe the most valuable aspect of the sacrament of penance is in its anonymity and strict confidentiality. In many cases, the rule of confessional privilege forbids judicial inquiry into communications made under the seal of confession.

Upon entering the church, a parishioner selected one of six confessionals made available for that evening. When unoccupied, one would open a thick mahogany door, left or right, leaving the center compartment for the priest, who has the authority to absolve our sins.

Some lines were significantly shorter than others, depending on what priest had his name above the confessional. On most evenings, Father Anderson's line was virtually nonexistent. Although my academic performance may have been dismal, I was smart enough to know not to get into that line.

When parishioners enter a chamber, they may sit on a small wooden bench or stand in the darkness, waiting for the priest to open a veiled slot in the partition, indicating it was showtime. This method was super-efficient in getting us sinners in and out as quickly as possible.

After closing one slot, the priest shifts positions and opens the one on the other side to begin anew. The parishioner initiates his or her confession by saying, "Bless me, Father, for I have sinned. It has been one week, one month, or like me, 41.5 years since my last confession, and these are my sins."

After acknowledging your recent bad behavior, the priest asks you to recite the Act of Contrition, a traditional post-confessional prayer. I remember it like this: "Oh my God, I am heartily sorry for having offended thee. And I detest all my sins because of thy just punishment. Most of all, because they offend thee, my God, who art all good and deserving of all my love."

For your penance, the priest may instruct you to recite some additional prayers in the sanctuary before leaving the church. He blesses you with the sign of the cross and says, "Your sins are forgiven. Go in peace and sin no more." I remember sometimes leaving the confessional feeling somewhat cleansed—until I walked out of the church and hit the streets. Who knows? If the church administered this sacrament every four to six hours as doctors prescribe antibiotics, I could have been saved.

Our school's next mandatory confession occurred a week after my infamous "dirty dozen detention day." As our class marched into the church, Sister Mary Frances, perched on a platform overlooking the sanctuary, directed us to which confessional we were to go. My karma must have sucked back then. As I made it to the front of the line, Sister Mary Frances pointed left, indicating that I should head over to Father Anderson's confessional.

This selection process reminds me of the one Viktor Frankl describes in his book, *Man's Search for Meaning*. In this masterpiece of psychological insight, Frankl discovers the transformational ability of those torn apart from their previous existence and put into the most horrifying circumstances. As a Jew in Nazi Germany, Frankl and his family were rounded up and sent to different concentration camps throughout Germany and Poland.

The destination for Viktor Frankl was the Nazi's notorious death camp, Auschwitz. Frankl's fellow prisoners warned him there would be a "selection process" as they passed through the gate. If the officer in charge believed you were healthy enough to perform heavy labor, he pointed to the right. If he indicated for you to go left, you went directly to the gas chambers and crematorium. I recently visited Auschwitz and stood in the exact spot where this selection process took place.

As I sat and waited for Father Anderson to begin, I was shaking like a leaf. I had no idea what to say but knew I better think of something quick. When he opened the slot on my side of the confessional, I developed speech impediments I never knew I had.

I lied from the get-go, telling the good padre it was only one week since my last confession.

I could sense he already knew it was me lying again on the other side of the wall. I confessed I used foul language several times; I had a fistfight in the schoolyard with one of my classmates and stole a *Playboy* magazine hidden in my father's closet. I thought my confession was going reasonably well until I mentioned the thing about the magazine.

Like a wounded grizzly bear, Father Anderson roared, "Whaaaaaaat!" I was yanked out of the confessional by the collar of my shirt and dragged up to the altar, where he instructed me to kneel and not move until he finished hearing everyone's confession. I believed my karma might have improved somewhat when an hour or so later, Father Anderson walked up to me and said in an uncharacteristically soft voice, "Go home and have your mother call me."

To me, this indicated one of two possibilities. Either Father Anderson was going to let me go scot-free, or I was in deep trouble. Would anyone care to venture a guess on what happens next?

Thank God for mothers. I believe the good padre felt compassion toward my mother for being a single parent of five children. My mom also volunteered for the Rosary Society, which, among other things, was responsible for soliciting donations for the church. My mom said she had to beg Father Anderson not to expel me from school. She did so by reminding him that I would be in high school and out of his hair forever in a few short months.

Father Anderson agreed to keep me in school but cautioned, "If I ever hear a peep out of him," you know the rest. Blah, blah, blah, blah, blah, blah, blah. I realize, at least up to that point, I did not qualify to be labeled a true sociopath. I may not have done so well academically, but I was smart enough to know that until graduation day, I had to become like all three monkeys: see no evil, hear no evil, and peep no evil.

# 7

# CHEERS TO HIGHER EDUCATION

F OR A FEW BRIEF MOMENTS DURING THE SUMMER OF 1970, I felt I might not be on God's hit list for hell after all. My two biggest tormentors, my biological father and Father Anderson, were no longer active participants in my nightmares. Could it be the personality kid had finally got a break in life? I am sure you all heard the saying, "Be careful of what you pray for; you just might get it." Well, I got it, all right—out of the frying pan and into the fire I went.

As my older brother was an alumnus, I got accepted into one of the country's most prestigious high schools. The Brothers, who ran this all-boy school of excellence, assured my mother I would fit right in. They explained a significant number of their students lived in single-parent homes in tough neighborhoods throughout the city. This school's credo was "Changing boys into men." All I could say was, *Jesus, Mary, and Joseph, what the hell am I doing in a place like this?*

This school provided an excellent education without consideration of the family's economic status. In the 1970s, the demographics of the upper west side of Manhattan changed. Most of my fellow students traveled up from Brooklyn and down from Harlem and the Bronx, and I was a skinny, freckle-faced little white boy from Queens. For the first time, I got a taste of what it must feel like to be a minority in this country. And for the record, it sucks.

There was a new nemesis in town, who held the title "Dean of Discipline" at the school. His mission was to catch those students violating any of the school's regulations. Without much imagination, it was easy to picture this maniacal disciple of discipline dressed in black leather, moonlighting as a bouncer in one of the S&M clubs on Bleeker Street.

I read an article indicating that only 7% of Americans found personal satisfaction in their employment. Our dear Dean of Discipline was undoubtedly one of those. His joy came by dressing up in various disguises and hiding behind newspapers and magazines in archways and storefronts throughout the neighborhood. Whenever he saw one of us breaking any of the school's regulations, he would come out of hiding, happy as a clam as he wrote our names in his little black book.

During my first week of school, the bell rang for a first-period gym class. As I was running a few minutes late and did not want to get punished for it, I cut class altogether. Like most of my decisions back then, this one did not go quite as planned.

At this school, detention consisted of coming in on Saturday mornings and sitting quietly at your desk for three hours. Or you could volunteer to do an hour of general maintenance work around the school. I had to show up for the next ten Saturdays in a row for cutting this one class. I believed those in authority gave out such harsh punishments to develop a slave labor pool capable of maintaining their dilapidated half-century-old building.

I completed my freshman and sophomore years at this "Escola de excelência," but as the Good Book says, there is a time for all seasons. There is a time to live and a time to die. A time to sow and a time to reap. A time to stay and a time to get the hell out of Dodge. I informed my mother that if I could not switch schools for my junior and senior years, I would drop out altogether.

As usual, my mom pulled some strings and got me into a progressive, artsy school less than a mile from our home. Instead of taking a train into Manhattan six days a week, it was now only a short walk to school. Most of our teachers were as laidback as you could get. Students could wear ripped-up jeans, T-shirts, and flip-flops, even in the winter, if so desired. If you turned in all your assignments on time, some teachers did not require you to attend their classes. Boo-yah!

The 1960s turned into the 70s without much fanfare for me. With its epicenter in the Haight-Ashbury district of San Francisco, the hippie movement continued to inspire young people throughout the country. Bands like the Grateful Dead, Jefferson Airplane, Pink Floyd, the Jimi Hendrix Experience, and the Beatles ushered in a new music genre called "psychedelic rock."

The drug culture showed no signs of slowing down. Timothy Leary, a nationally known psychologist, advocated for the use of LSD for recreational use. He suggested that all young people should "Turn on, tune in, and drop out." Dr. Leary implied that LSD was a dream come true but failed to acknowledge it could also be your worst nightmare. I experienced both.

The first time I tried LSD, I swallowed a little yellow tablet inscribed with LSD-25 on one side. The federal government issued these tablets for the sole purpose of scientific research, but somehow, they found their way into our hands. The government's formula was in its purest form and offered a colorful and serene out-of-body experience. Finally, our government got something right. God bless America!

Within a few short months, LSD was being synthetically made in garages and distributed by diehard hippies everywhere. This product required one to lick the drug, produced in liquid form, off a piece of paper the size of a postage stamp. As this product was invisible, we were never sure how much of it we were taking. But whatever amount I took on a snowy winter's day, it was way too much.

Later that evening, home alone and out of my mind, I called one of my old school counselors and begged him for help. Father McGregor, referred to by some as "the junkie priest" and by many as a modern-day St. Francis of Assisi, dropped whatever he was doing and drove from Manhattan to Queens to help.

His last words to me over the telephone were, "Before you do anything else, unlock your door so that I can get in."

When my angel arrived, I was sitting with my legs dangling out my bedroom window, not wanting to jump but intent on flying. I told this story to my family for the first time during our reunion in Cancun. My sister said she remembered that night very well. When she returned home from school that evening, she found a suicide note I left on the dining room table. Father McGregor saved my life that day—one of many days, my life would need saving.

I made a pact with one of my good friends in high school to meet up every morning before school to smoke a fat one. During first-period psychology, my friend Rick and I looked at each other and realized we did not get high that morning. Simultaneously, we got out of our seats and walked out of class. We went straight into the bathroom and smoked a bowl of fine Turkish hashish.

When we returned to our seats, the entire class started laughing when the teacher pulled an oversized magnifying glass out of his desk and called us up to the front of the classroom. He told us to keep our eyes wide open and invited every student to come up to see "The bloodshot eyes of people who habitually smoke marijuana."

Soon after graduation, Rick married his childhood sweetheart. Shortly after they married, Rick got high for the last time. He fell off a roof and died of his injuries. I think of Rick often and wish him well on his journey.

# 8

# McGUINEA-MAGOO

WHILE VACATIONING IN RIO DE JANEIRO, BRAZIL, I had the opportunity to experience the sheer beauty and majesty of Ipanema and Copacabana Beach. Looking down from that iconic 125-foot statue of Jesus, *Cristo Redentor* (Christ the Redeemer), you see one of the most incredible vistas and some of the most expensive real estate on the planet. If you were to turn 180 degrees and look upward, you would be facing Rocinha, one of Brazil's largest favelas.

In Brazil, the only Portuguese-speaking country in South America, *favela* describes what South Africans refer to as shantytowns, and Americans call slums or ghettos. These mob-administered, crime-infested neighborhoods stretch as far as the eye can see in coastal cities throughout Brazil.

Can you imagine being the parent of a hungry child living in Rocinha looking down upon such affluence? Most of us who are parents would be thinking the same thing, whether we believe in

Jesus or not. When our children are going to bed hungry, we will make deals with the devil we would never consider under any other circumstance.

In the movie *Wall Street*, Gordon, the character of Michael Douglas, is an ambitious stockbroker who would do anything to climb to the top. This movie is best known when Gordon stood up at a stockholder's meeting and proclaimed, "Greed is good." I do not believe greed is good but having enough food to feed your family is another story.

Unless the courts pressured my father to pay his fair share or go to jail, child support remained just another one of his good intentions. Our mother was too proud to ask for public assistance, so she worked full time during the day and had a part-time job in the evening. In between the two, she would return home, feed us, and get us ready for school the next day. On weekends, she did freelance typing and crocheted hats that sold for five bucks a pop.

I believe I did everything a teenager could do to add a few bucks to the family's coffers. Every day I got up at five a.m. to complete my paper route before heading off for school. I gathered discarded bottles from the alleyways and our garden area to collect the deposits made on them. In the winter, I sold Christmas trees and shoveled snow. I moved furniture, swept floors, and usually hung around construction sites looking for a few hours of work.

One of the more lucrative gigs I had was after I made a wooden shoeshine box I took into the neighborhood bars late in the evenings. In these later hours, the customers were more intoxicated and vulnerable to a bright-eyed, freckle-faced little boy who had any number of sad stories to tell. By pulling some sleight of hand, I could make anyone who had a few too many have nothing left by the time he left the bar.

I could have gravitated toward any number of neighborhood cliques, but I was not very athletic, so I did not fit in with the jocks. I felt no connection whatsoever with the intellectuals. The groups I identified with were the misfits and street punks who dropped out of school, used drugs, and committed street-level crimes to support their habits.

I somehow felt a deep connection with a group of middle-aged Italian men who gathered at Sal's, a neighborhood sweet shop and newspaper stand. These were the guys I looked up to as a kid. They were the men who operated out in the open without fear of the local police.

They were not the character types you would find in *The Godfather, The Sopranos*, or *Goodfellas*. In 2019 I watched a few episodes of *The Deuce,* which premiered in 2017 on HBO. This show was spot on from my perspective, hustling the street of New York in the 1970s. There was one exception; we never got involved in prostitution. The one thing we did have back then was respect for women.

In 1970, the RICO Act (racketeer influenced and corrupt organizations) became law and forever changed how the mobsters conducted business on the streets. This bill allowed federal prosecution and extended criminal penalties for racketeering activities performed as part of an ongoing criminal enterprise.

Sal did not seem interested in whether he sold any merchandise in the store or not. Most days, you found him and a rotating group of middle-aged men playing pinochle over the soda counter. Seizing the opportunity, I began greeting customers, selling newspapers and cigarettes, making milkshakes, egg creams, and banana splits every chance I got. Without much opposition, I wiggled my way into becoming the store's new soda jerk. Most of the men who filtered in and out of the store did not seem the least bit interested in playing cards. Their game was running numbers, narcotics trafficking, loan sharking, counterfeiting, and credit card fraud. The ladder would prove to be their downfall.

One day Sal introduced me to a well-dressed, heavyset gentleman who marched into the store ranting and raving about what, I do not know. The characteristics I remember most about this guy was his severely pockmarked face and piercing dark eyes, devoid of any life.

He appeared flustered and a bit on the paranoid side. I stood in the back of the store, cleaning and stocking shelves, hoping to stay out of the drama.

He stared at me for quite a while before turning to Sal. "What the hell is this kid doing here? He's not even Italian."

Sal responded, "I know, he's Irish, but we keep around because he's funny."

The man half smiled and said, "Oh, so he's a McGuinea." That was the term he used for an Irish wannabe-Italian.

My all-time favorite movie growing up was *the St. Valentine's Day Massacre*, which debuted in theaters in 1967. This film sheds light on the real-life turf war between Al "Scarface" Capone (played by Jason Robards) and his lifelong nemesis George "Bugs" Moran for control of Chicago's lucrative bootlegging, gambling, and prostitution business.

Their bloody conflict played out on the streets of Chicago, reaching a climax when seven of Capone's men, some dressed in police uniforms, raided Moran's garage on the north side of Chicago. Everyone in the garage, including an accountant, was lined up facing a wall. Capone's men, using machine-guns, shotguns, and pistols, shot and killed everyone on St. Valentine's Day, 1929.

Over time, my Italian friends no longer walked into the back-storage area to talk business. Having earned the trust of these men opened a whole new world of possibilities for me. In the beginning, I ran errands and picked up loan payments from local shop owners. Within months, I drove uptown with Sal and his cousin Vinny delivering small glassine envelopes to dealers impatiently waiting in dimly lit hallways.

Sal believed the police would never suspect that a thin, freckle-faced little boy was delivering bundles of heroin in East Harlem. He assured me because of my age, I would not be sent to prison and promised to pay for an attorney if I ever got busted.

However, he warned me if I ever touched what was inside those bags, he would put a cap in my head. I felt like Sal was counseling me about the dangers of heroin the same way a loving father would advise his son about the inherent risks of driving.

Most days, I got home from school and changed from my torn-up jeans and T-shirt into a gray suit, white shirt, and necktie. Since this was the only suit I had, I wore it every time I went out collecting envelopes. It felt odd to have grown men, with tears in their eyes, pleading with me, a teenager, to convince "my boss" they would have the rest of his money within days.

My friends also found legitimate work for me as a transporter at a cement company and as a busboy in upscale restaurants and catering halls throughout Queens. While bussing tables, I looked for the more mature, unaccompanied women tapping their feet to the beat of the music during wedding receptions.

I would take off my waiter's jacket and lead my princess up to the dance floor. Dancing the Lindy to the sounds of the Glen Miller Band usually earned the personality kid an extra twenty bucks by the end of the night. We now had fresh meat, fish, and produce on the table, and our gas, electric, and phone services never were disconnected again.

One day I was sent out to make a donut run for the boys. I was delighted when the girl behind the counter put an extra doughnut in my box, calling it a "baker's dozen." When I returned to the store, I suggested the group incorporate this concept of the baker's dozen into their narcotics business.

I explained they could put the same amount of product in thirteen bags instead of the standard twelve. This way, their customers would believe they were getting an extra bag of dope, when in fact, it would be the same old, same old.

This concept increased overall production and their bottom line. I believe in appreciation; I interviewed for a waiter's position at the Copacabana in New York City. The Copa was where legends like Frank Sinatra, Dean Martin, Tony Bennett, and Sammy Davis Jr. performed regularly.

That night, since I was only sixteen, too young to be served alcohol, I sipped tea while watching Dionne Warwick perform some of her hit songs that included "Do You Know the Way to San Jose?" "Walk on By," and "Alfie."

Toward the end of my senior year in high school, two new guys recently released from prison started showing up at the store. Consuming large quantities of amphetamines, these men were volatile and unpredictable. One day, as I walked into the store, the younger and more menacing of the two grabbed a handful of darts off the shelf. He gave me a count of three and then let them fly. I wish I had paid more attention to track and field in my freshman and sophomore years. If I did, I might not have become the human porcupine I did on that day.

One evening as the store was about to close, the men gathered outside, waiting for me to finish cleaning up. As I walked out, they were laughing like a pack of hyenas after a kill. I asked what was going on, and Sal told me to cross the street, which I did without question.

When I asked a second time, Sal, who was now taking large quantities of amphetamines himself, pulled a snub-nose 38 caliber revolver from his waistband and told me to run.

Run, I did. That evening, even Forrest Gump would have been proud of my sprinting abilities.

Unfortunately, bullets travel much faster than Forest or I could ever run. Sal fired three consecutive rounds, all of which ricocheted off a brick wall ten feet behind me. I ran the entire way home, never once looking back. As I sat on my couch trying to catch my breath, I thought to myself, m*an, that shit was not funny.*

I needed to find a way out of this madness before I was killed or sent to prison. The two new guys took a leading role in planning the next heist. This time they were not interested in just boosting items to sell on the streets; they wanted to empty the safe. These lunatics packed heat, and I believed they would not hesitate to use their guns if it meant going back to prison. Carrying firearms was a new phenomenon within the group, and I wanted no part of it.

After school one day, I was on my way to attend a scheduled meeting with the boys when a car came screeching to a halt beside me. One of the new guys jumped out of the back, picked me up, and planted me in the front passenger seat. I would be riding shotgun that day. Within seconds I got pistol-whipped on the left side of my head and face. I was one scared little boy as everyone in the car was screaming at the top of their lungs.

Thank God, my running partner Freddy was also in the car that evening. He managed to grab hold of this out-of-control fruitcake before he rendered me unconscious. You may ask, what did I do to make these guys so angry? On that day, I stayed after school to speak to one of my teachers about an assignment I needed to turn in the following day. The ensuing drama was all because I was twenty minutes late for the meeting.

The end finally came when federal agents raided the homes of those involved in the credit card scheme. The only woman on the crew, a platinum blonde bombshell, purchased everything from bubblegum to refrigerators with stolen credit cards. She liked me to come along so she would appear more like a typical housewife. She was a true professional, an artist in the field of deception.

They were all charged with possession of stolen merchandise and credit card fraud. I later heard Freddy also faced charges of selling Uzi submachine guns to undercover agents. The evening before the raid, one of the local shop owners, a loyal friend of the family, pulled me aside and suggested I disappear for a few days.

I took his advice and stayed disconnected, not only for a few days but for the next few years. I returned home only once to attend the funeral services of the best man at my wedding. When I left Queens, my good friend Steve was a committed pacifist. As I was chilling in the outskirts of New York, this gentle soul began robbing people by knifepoint to feed his heroin addiction. I still find this one hard to believe. This disease is powerful beyond measure.

Steve jumped out of his twenty-six-story office building window after being called into his boss's office and terminated from his job. He landed headfirst onto the hard concrete below, suffering catastrophic injuries, killing him instantly. His was a closed-casket service. All the king's horses and all the king's men could not put my friend Steve back together again.

As a kid, one of my favorite cartoon characters was the lovable elder statesman Quincy Magoo. Although Mr. Magoo wore thick, coke-bottle glasses, he was still as blind as a bat. Due to his severe nearsightedness and stubbornness to go it alone, Mr. Magoo found himself in all sorts of dire straits.

You would typically see him walking onto a moving beam at a construction site. But just before he stepped off the edge, someone or something would appear in the nick of time and guide him to safety. It seems good old Quincy and I had a lot in common. Don't you think?

# 9

# THE STRAW THAT BROKE THE ADDICTS BACK

ONE OF THE MORE RESPECTED NEUROLOGISTS IN SAN Diego examined me to help diagnose a plethora of bizarre symptoms affecting the muscle groups in my lower legs. According to Wikipedia, "Fasciculations are the synchronous contraction of all muscle fibers within a single unit." These fasciculations (abnormal muscle twitching) have gotten progressively worse and are now present 24/7 without reprieve.

My doctor took his usual in-depth medical history, but this time his focus was on my distant past. If you remember, I have shied away from discussing that part of my life with anyone. For the first time, I felt my past finally caught up with me and was responsible for some of the symptoms I was now experiencing.

Since forced to retire early due to medical issues, I finally felt free to answer all the doctor's questions as truthfully as possible. In the middle of the interview, he looked up from his notes, shook his head, and said, "Man, cats ain't got nothing on you." His comments were in direct response to the number of times he felt I had cheated death.

I nodded, acknowledging my awareness of how lucky I am to be alive. When I first got clean, I remember simultaneously feeling both grateful and guilty. That out of the many, I had been given another chance to live.

In our teens, a neighborhood friend and classmate, Antonio, a.k.a. "The Monk," made it to our local newspaper's front page. The caption read "Crime Spree Lands Teen in Jail." On one of the busiest intersections in Queens, Antonio held up one store after another, taking the entire metal trays out of the registers.

Antonio was carrying several of these trays when arrested. Think of the mentality of a person capable of doing such a brazen act in broad daylight. As Mr. Rogers would say, it was just another wonderful day in the neighborhood.

Antonio got remanded to New York's infamous Riker's Island but received an early release due to overcrowding. Back on the streets, he was re-arrested and convicted of shooting an acquaintance through the neck at point-blank range. He was sent back to Riker's, where his father worked as a corrections officer. You cannot make this stuff up, folks.

Antonio broke out of Riker's by sneaking onto a civilian bus leaving the compound. New York's Finest cornered him in a community laundry room a short time later, on the same block where he lived. They planted listening devices and waited for him to fall asleep. They captured him without a struggle—or a stitch of clothing on his body.

Sitting in a police cruiser covered only by a blanket, a news reporter asked him, "With all the legal repercussions you will be facing, was your escape worth it for just a couple hours of freedom?"

Antonio looked directly into the camera and said in the most stereotypical New York accent, "Of course it was worth it. I had a fantastic time." And my friends called me psycho?

My principal purpose for writing this book was to offer hope to those suffering directly or indirectly from the horrors of addiction, in whatever form it takes. To this end, I want to limit my writing about what chemicals I used, how I used them, or any of my criminal behavior and focus on the all-important why I felt the need to self-destruct. If we do not understand why addicts feel the need to use, we will never help anyone, including ourselves, find long-lasting recovery.

Why would someone appearing normal in every other way willingly take deadly poisons, knowing it is the common denominator to why their lives are spinning out of control? The bewildered parents of addicted children will often cry out, "Don't they realize how much we love them?" Unfortunately, addiction can and will often trump even the power of love. For this reason, the first step in any recovery process must be absolute and unconditional surrender.

We all heard reports of children abandoned or even sold by their strung-out parents. Men and women, hitting their knees for a hit of crack that will only satisfy their cravings for a few euphoric moments. But if you believe heroin is found only in economically depressed neighborhoods, you better think again. Since 2015, opiate consumption has grown exponentially in small-town, middle-class America. As Dorothy would say after arriving in the land of Oz, "We're not in Kansas anymore," my friends.

As you must have already concluded, I am a very handsome, intelligent, spiritual, well-established, well-disciplined, successful, kind, loving, compassionate, lucky, empathetic, understanding, funny, grateful, generous, and most importantly, a very humble man. So keeping true to form, I would like to repost some of my more brilliant concepts about addiction I shared with you earlier. Worry not, my friends; I will be writing extensively about our self-centered nature in future chapters.

I do not believe genetics plays a predominant role in why some of us will develop chemical dependencies. I think it is the psychosocial atmosphere we find ourselves in without acquiring the necessary skills to cope. No matter the stimulus, the underlying cause of addiction is a spiritual void that drives those addicted to numb their emotional pain no matter the cost.

Whenever I speak on this subject, it is typical for someone in the audience to approach me later and say, "Great message, Sean, but I do not think you understand the gravity of my situation. I have lost everything—my wife and children, my friends, my employment—and I wake up feeling sick as a dog every day. What did you do, smoke pot on the weekends? Have a few beers with the boys?"

One day, a nurse noticed me walking out of our storage area, carrying several boxes of syringes, heading to the Operating Room, and asked where I was taking them. To the bathroom, I said, to shoot some dope. She laughed and said, "Sean, you are the happiest person I know and the last person on earth that would do such a thing." I smiled back and thought, *My God, if she only knew!*

And yes, I smoked pot, but unlike Bill Clinton, I inhaled as deeply as possible. And yes, I drank alcohol, having my first blackout before my thirteenth birthday. I took various hallucinogens, ingested every type of upper and downer that hit the streets, and mainlined heroin and cocaine.

I spent eight years of my life a prisoner on the methadone maintenance program. I have been locked up and earned frequent-flier miles for my many visits to various institutions. I believe I have the right to say to anyone suffering from any manifestation of this disease, I understand.

It may surprise you, but it was not my chemical intake that brought me to my knees but the insanity that comes with it. Some define insanity as "Doing the same thing over and over and expecting different results." If you never witnessed an addict going through opiate withdrawal, watch Jamie Foxx, in his Academy Award-winning portrayal of Ray Charles, in the movie "Ray" alone in his bedroom kicking heroin.

If you have an interest in understanding why addiction is called a "family disease," there is a fantastic show called *Addicted* (on Amazon

Prime), starring Kristina Wandzilak, which I highly recommend. Kristina, a recovering addict herself and now an interventionist, helps families understand the nature of addiction and begin the process of healing. This show is as real as it gets, folks. If you are an addict or a family member with a desire to help someone you love, *Addicted* is must-see TV.

The last time I found myself locked behind bars was in the summer of 1976 while trying to score a few bags of dope on Ninth Street between avenues C and D in Alphabet City. There was a panic in the streets of New York. Heroin was a precious commodity.

On a muggy Sunday afternoon, I stood in line for well over an hour, waiting for my connection to show up. In line with me were men and women in business attire, two Hasidic Jews dressed in their full orthodox regalia, and several other street punks just like me looking for a fix.

Suddenly, all the locals disappeared into the abandoned buildings on both sides of the block. As I stood there trying to grasp the situation, six men came hauling ass down the middle of Ninth Street. I should have realized right away this was a bust, but when you are dope sick, you are focused on one thing and one thing only, getting well again.

The first question the undercover agent who placed me under arrest asked, "Are you stupid? Didn't you see when we rolled up, everyone on the block ran, except for you idiots?"

My best apologies had no positive effect on the officer. I was cuffed and taken to central booking, eventually ending up in "The Tombs," a detention complex in lower Manhattan, for the rest of the evening. Fortunately, the courts ruled this kind of street sweeping unconstitutional, and I left the court the next day a free man.

The epitome of my drug-induced insanity came on a day when I purchased a gram of cocaine from a local dealer. He warned me to be careful as this cocaine was "as close to pure as you can get." But dealers all say the same bull; that their dope is the best out there. After all, like in any business, they want you to purchase their product and not their competitors'.

I raced home, locked myself in the bathroom, put half the cocaine into the cooker (usually a bent spoon or bottle cap), and let it fly. Within seconds, I knew whatever amount I just injected; was way too much. As I was losing consciousness, I prayed that God would not let me die on this day, in this manner, on my bathroom floor. My poor mother would be the one to find me dead, with a spike in my arm.

As I regained consciousness, my body was convulsing, my clothes drenched in sweat. There was blood and vomit splattered everywhere. The rig (needle and syringe) was now lying in the bathtub, unbloodied and blameless as if it did not play any role whatsoever in my near-death experience.

When I gained enough strength, I sat on the toilet and thanked God I was still alive. However, I quickly remembered I still had half the cocaine left in my pocket, and the usual "addict's debate" ensued. One side insisting I shoot the rest of the cocaine, a.s.a.p., while the other reminded me if I did not wait at least a couple of hours, I would not experience the same intense "rush" I had earlier. Would anyone care to venture a guess on what happens next?

It took fewer than ten minutes to have the rest of the cocaine flowing through my veins. This level of insanity is almost impossible to comprehend for those who are not addicted. Family and friends will wonder why their loved ones cannot muster up enough willpower to stop using. However, trying to control addiction by will power alone is like trying to redirect diarrhea in midstream: it's not going to happen!

As I mentioned earlier, I spent eight years of my life in a virtual coma being "maintained" on methadone. The good thing about methadone is it does stop your cravings for heroin and may keep you out of jail. However, methadone is a much more physically addictive drug than heroin. After being on methadone for several months, addicts will no longer feel the buzz they desire. They will now need to pursue other methods to fill the void.

I began taking ethchlorvynol, a pharmaceutical drug no longer available on the market. My dealer, who was in line with me at the clinic, said these oversized green 750 mg gel tabs were "used to tranquilize horses."

I said, "Really? If they are good enough to put down a horse, then they are good enough for me. I'll take a dozen."

After abusing this drug for several years, I began to lose touch with reality. One day, while standing in line at the clinic, the head nurse overheard me telling some of my fellow "Methadonians" about my ability to separate my soul from my body. Within hours she had me admitted for detox and observation at a nearby hospital on the lower East Side.

I have landed in some scary places before, but nothing like this. Behind the locked doors of this raggedy-ass detox center, fear, tears, and despair reigned supreme. Most patients in the ward were convicted felons sent here to detox before being sent to prisons throughout New York State.

Out of the ninety-bed population, I was one of two patients with seizure precaution signs and tongue depressors plastered around our beds. Could it be that the Personality Kid was sicker than those patients doing the "Thorazine shuffle" up and down the corridors? I was about to find out just how ill I was.

After hearing researchers discovered that cockroaches communicate with each other the same way ants do, instead of killing them outright, I captured them, broke their hind legs, and placed them behind the refrigerator. I reasoned the wounded bugs would warn the others that a madman was waiting for them outside to do more of the same. I continue to believe this is the best method we have for eradicating insects in our homes today. Come on, guys. I'm only kidding.

Most worrisome, months after my discharge from the hospital, I was still having auditory hallucinations, hearing arrows whizzing past my right ear. Now, even my friends started crossing the street when they saw me coming. Eventually, a small amount of blood-tinged pus begun oozing out of my ear. Upon investigating, I pulled out a broken piece of a Q-tip that looked like it had been in my ear for decades. Left in this state, I believe it would have been more humane if my family took me to the ASPCA and euthanized.

# 10

# NEVER ALONE

THE MONTH I SPENT IN DETOX WAS THE LAST TIME I
ever needed to be institutionalized due to chemical dependency.
More than a year after discharge, I was still only getting four or five
hours of sleep a night, but that was two or three more hours than
I was getting six months prior. Everything around me was starting
to get noticeably better. It was hard to identify at first, but I was
beginning to feel something I never experienced before: It was hope!

On those sleepless nights, I spent most of my time watching the
tube until all thirteen channels we had back then signed off for the
evening. I would then sit for hours on my mother's balcony, staring
into the darkness of the ocean and empty streets below.

It was for these precious few hours of sleep and the ability to
move my bowels again without the use of laxatives for which I was
most grateful. No one told me when I started using narcotics; I would
be shooting moon rocks out of my ass for years to come.

In the months leading up to 1985, I believed I was doing

reasonably well. I worked in a well-respected profession, opened bank accounts, and received credit cards in my name only. For the first time in my life, I lived by myself and paid all my bills on time. I started writing and performing some of my original songs with my younger brother's new wave/punk rock band. I was beginning to feel alive again!

But as the saying goes, "All good things must come to an end." You could put a tuxedo on a monkey, but at the end of the night, when the party's over, you are still going home with a monkey. I stayed away from using any "heavy drugs" until the beginning of 1985, when, for no apparent reason, I began to monkey around again.

This time, even I could see how quickly my disease was progressing, and it scared the living hell out of me. I knew from experience that losing my job and being disconnected from my family and friends were right around the corner. I could not bear telling my mother that once again, I screwed up. So I did something I never did before; I turned myself in.

As I searched everywhere for help, flyers started showing up all over the hospital where I worked. A new employee assistance program became available for anyone needing assistance dealing with life on life's terms. They promised strict confidentiality unless you were a danger to yourself, your coworkers or jeopardized patient safety in any way.

Since I did not have a physical dependency on any substance, my counselor at the EAP felt I could participate in the program on an outpatient basis. To my great surprise, he allowed me to continue working. He suggested that, along with counseling and therapy, I regularly attend twelve-step meetings. I knew his suggestions were not suggestions; I needed to do everything he asked if I wanted to keep my job.

My first meeting was in a small Lutheran Church a short distance from home. Like most newcomers, I sat in the back, kept my sunglasses on, and did not say a word to anyone. That evening, the speaker was a war-torn looking woman in her mid-thirties with sparkling blue eyes and platinum-blonde hair. When queued, she walked up to the podium and introduced herself by saying, "My name is Gabby, and I am an addict."

There was something extraordinary about this woman. Although she had cavernous track marks (overused injection sites) running up and down her arms, none of her tracks were fresh. This woman appeared genuinely happy and at peace. When she said she recently celebrated three years clean (total abstinence from all drugs), I thought to myself, *My God, is this possible?*

Gabby went on to say if she could do it, anyone could do it. "Once an addict, always an addict is dead," she said. She suggested newcomers attend ninety meetings in their first ninety days and stay away from the people, places, and things that trigger our compulsion to use. She also suggested we get a sponsor, someone to talk to, one on one, for extra strength and guidance.

I received many well-meaning suggestions from the group that evening but did not listen to any of them. "Make ninety meetings in ninety days?" These people need to get a life. "Complete abstinence from all drugs?" My only problem was with opiates. "Stay away from people, places, and things?" Impossible; my entire life revolved around my getting and using and finding ways to get more. "Call another man and talk about my feelings?" What a ridiculous concept that is!

So I ran the program the way I thought it should run—my way. I went to three meetings the first week, two the second and did not ask anyone to sponsor me. I did not stay away from people, places, and things. I continued to drink alcohol, smoke pot, and only spoke to the women attending the meetings.

Somehow I managed to stop using any "heavy drugs" for a couple of weeks. But on a hot summer day without rhyme or reason, I bought a single bag of heroin from a local dealer who had yellow pus oozing from an abscess on his left forearm. As soon as we made the exchange, all the hope I previously felt by attending the meetings came to a screeching halt.

I remembered an old scripture saying, "It is better to be ignorant than to have seen the light and go back into darkness." There are only two mistakes an addict can make in recovery. The first is not starting the process, and the second is not coming back if you relapse.

Ashamed, humiliated, and once again feeling like a failure, I returned to the meetings the very next day. It was on that day I learned the true meaning of surrender.

Gabby, who was also at that meeting, ran up to me, gave me a big hug, and said, "Welcome home, Sean," three words that would forever change my life.

Now, not only did I hear the suggestions the group was making, but I began to practice them as if my life depended on it. That night I walked up to a serene-looking gentleman and asked if he would be my sponsor. I told him I would do everything he suggested and meant every word I said. That was my moment of clarity, a place of absolute unconditional surrender.

Ray was around my age, knew what it was like being strung out on heroin, and had more than three years clean. But before he gave me the official thumbs-up, he asked if I would make ninety meetings in ninety days and call him regularly? I assured him I would do anything he suggested if it would help me stay clean.

After agreeing to be my sponsor, Ray suggested I find a home group, a meeting I would attend every week, and become a trusted servant of that group. I did just that and became the official coffee maker, a step up from my previous position as the candy store's soda jerk.

This commitment required me to get there early to make the coffee and stay late to clean up the mess. In-kind, it forced me to become vulnerable and get to know the other members of the group. Being of service remains the cornerstone of my recovery today.

I know for those who are not addicted, these suggestions must seem simple and easy to accomplish. Imagine, however, at the age of ten, you fell into a deep coma and woke twenty years later, unfamiliar with anything you have previously known. Your mental capacity, emotional stability, and relationship skills remained dormant during that entire time. That was my reality, and it was terrifying. Nothing was simple; nothing was easy!

The suggestion I found most challenging was staying away from people, places, and things. Everyone I knew used something. What would it be like hanging out with friends, listening to music, and eating Twinkies without being wasted? As I was doing everything I could to stay clean, some of my "friends" were doing everything they could to get me loaded again. For the most part, skillful avoidance and some low-level threats made these pests go away.

Unfortunately, one of my coworkers could not seem to take no for an answer. One day as we were changing back into our street clothes, he told me he just scored, and since we were such good friends, he would give me my first hit for free. I lost it. I picked him up and slammed him against his locker. I told him if he even mentions rolling paper to me again, I will slit his blankety-blank throat. This tactic worked quite well, and we never had to revisit this issue.

When I first started attending meetings, it felt like I was sitting in the middle of an insane asylum. We only had a limited number of members who managed to stay clean for multiple years. There was a feeling of desperation throughout our fellowship. Many of our members had secondary life-threatening illnesses. In the mid-1980s, those who developed AIDS often died from the virus within a year of diagnosis.

The New York Department of Health, located in an old clinically depressing building in lower Manhattan, was one of the only places in New York offering free testing. Everyone testing for the virus required counseling and a six-week waiting period before obtaining their results. Unfortunately, some who tested positive took their own lives soon after receiving their diagnosis.

After the phlebotomist drew my blood, I felt an urgent need to wash my hands. As I entered the graffiti-covered walls of the restroom, one specific area caught my attention. These are the words the author wrote verbatim: "I just found out I am HIV positive, and I am going to infect every motherf@cker I can." I am sure you do not need my analysis to feel the intensity of this man's rage. It was this level of raw emotion that was pervasive throughout our fellowship.

One evening, a friend also in recovery told me he was fooling around on his wife, who was at home taking care of their newborn. Cheating anyone out of anything, for whatever reason, is the antithesis of what we practice in recovery. My friend's affair was most disturbing, as I knew his wife and held their baby boy in my arms. When I asked if he used condoms with the other women, after a long awkward pause, he blurted out, "Come on, Sean, lighten up; we got to let loose sometimes."

At that moment, my friend was no longer a friend; he was an assassin. Even the most innocent among us can suffer the consequences of addiction. The parents of an angelic baby girl asked me to be one of the pallbearers at her funeral. At nine months old, she got diagnosed with HIV in utero, a term that would become all too familiar worldwide. Soon after her first birthday, this precious child of God succumbed to the virus.

The day of her funeral was one of the saddest I can remember. However, our fellowship packed the church to support the parents, Mike and Amber, who were devastated by their child's demise. I felt comfortable inserting the parents' names here as they both perished in the years following from the same disease they inflicted upon their daughter.

The seriousness of this disease became evident when, on November 20, 2015, Matt Lauer interviewed actor Charlie Sheen on NBC's *Today* show. Charlie came on the show to reveal he has been HIV positive for the past four years. Alongside Charlie was his physician, Dr. Robert Huizenga, who said, "My biggest concern with Charlie as a patient is substance abuse and depression, more than what HIV can do regarding shortening his life because it's not going to."

Dr. Huizenga's comments were great news for those infected with

HIV but a wake-up call for all of us directly or indirectly impacted by addiction. Dr. Drew, media personality and addiction medicine specialist, also commented on Charlie Sheen's status: "HIV is not a death sentence anymore. It is now a chronic disease like diabetes if you take your medicine on a regular basis. With HIV, you can live for thirty to forty years. With addiction, you're dead tomorrow."

Before putting pen to paper, I decided not to make the twelve steps the focus of my writings. There is an eclectic variety of books on the subject authored by individuals more qualified and articulate than I could ever be. Since 1939, the Twelve Steps, conceived by the founders of Alcoholics Anonymous, laid down a roadmap for recovery, which over the years has helped millions of people recover from the systematic torture of this hideous disease.

More than anything in recent memory, watching advertisements for a rehabilitation center located in Hoity-Toity-Town, California, made me sick to my stomach. One of the rehab's cofounders was trying to sell his concept of being "cured" from addiction while minimizing twelve-step programs. His revelation for the cure came from his father's counsel, who said he would need to determine why he used drugs if he ever wanted to be cured of his addiction. This revelation was about as innovative as the revelation I had this morning when I heard a little voice telling me I better get out of bed because I needed to pee.

This gentleman explained, "I like the idea of being cured as opposed to being forever an alcoholic, or forever an addict."

Well, golly, sir, I like the idea of Victoria's Secret supermodel Giselle leaving her husband, Tom Brady, for the likes of me. However, the odds of that happening are about the same as you "curing "an addict from addiction—nil to none!

Currently, a thirty-day program in Lalaland could cost upwards of $80,000. I am so incredibly grateful that I was never offered a "cure" for my addiction. By being "forever an addict," I did not have to mortgage my home. I did not have to max out my credit cards or sell any of my assets to discover why I used the way I used. Knowing this is a life-long process has encouraged me to continue working diligently on my recovery.

In the past thirty-five years, I have not paid one single penny to get clean, stay clean, and find peace of mind. The concept of being cured of addiction is absurd and against the medical community's beliefs worldwide. I hope I would never be so smug as to tell anyone where they should or should not go to find recovery. However, I would strongly suggest choosing a program rooted in spiritual principles, not based on profit.

Twelve-step fellowships work because the therapeutic value of one addict helping another is without parallel. Our members give it away to anyone reaching out for help without expecting anything in return. We volunteer to carry this life-saving message into hospitals, jails, and institutions. We believe everyone is salvageable, and no one need ever die of this disease.

If you are somehow concerned since I stopped using drugs, the second half of this book will not be as entertaining as the first; think again—some of the wackiest things I ever thought, said or did, accrued after I stopped getting loaded. So, hold on to your hats, for this story is just beginning!

# 11

# BROKEN MIRRORS

*GNÔTHI SEAUTON* (KNOW THYSELF) IS THE FIRST OF seven wise sayings inscribed in the temple of Apollo at Delphi. Socrates expanded on this concept by teaching, "The unexamined life is not worth living."

I want to start this chapter by asking three questions that have been pondered by scholars throughout the ages. Who am I? Why am I here? What is this presence I can sense but cannot see or touch?

Many of us will inevitably answer the second question by asking another: "Well, we are here to be happy, right?" Yes, I believe happiness is the endpoint of our journey for those who have come to know themselves. But when we are equivocal in our belief that we are here to be happy, we sentence the very thing we seek to a never-never land of wasted possibilities.

Mark Twain said, "The two most important days in your life are the day you were born, and the day you find out why." Despite all of man's accomplishments—flight, the automobile, electricity, incredible advances in medicine, global internet communication, and even placing a man on the moon—we still have not found a reliable way to tap into a loving heart. We may have accumulated all the gadgets advertisers tell us we need to be happy, but our dissatisfaction in life remains unchanged.

According to an old Hindu legend, there was a time when all men were gods but so abused their divinity that Brahma, the chief god, decided to take it away and hide it in a place where they would never find it. When the lesser gods were called in council to consider this question, they said, "We will bury man's divinity deep within the earth." But Brahma said, no, that will not do, for one day, man will dig deep into the earth.

The lesser gods spoke. "We will sink man's divinity into the deepest ocean." But again, Brahma replied, "No, for one day, man will learn to dive into the deepest of waters."

Then the lesser gods said, "We will take it to the top of the highest mountain, and there hide it." But again, Brahma replied," No, for man will eventually climb every mountain on earth."

Then Brahma said, "Here is what we will do with man's divinity. We will hide it deep within man himself, for he will never think to look for it there."

Since then, the legend concludes people have been searching, digging, climbing, and diving for something only found within themselves.

Sadly, this parable still rings true for most of us born into this self-absorbed, dog-eat-dog society. Most of us scurry about our lives, giving little or no thought as to why we do the things we do. We prance around like chickens without heads trying to find the ri person, the dream job, or that never-ending cash flow to reac elusive golden ring of contentment.

Whether we believe in a Supreme Being or not acknowledge there is both a human and a creati person. Most of us view ourselves as a physical quest instead of spiritual creatures having a human experience. Once again, we have it half-assed backward.

When we see ourselves as different, separate, and apart from our brothers and sisters, we set ourselves up for the pain, suffering, and disappointment that inherently exists within that illusion. When we choose to see life through the creative process, our lives seem to flow in a more fluid, peaceful, and positive direction. Let there be no misunderstanding; how we see ourselves and the world around us is created by design—our own.

The Sufi mystic Rumi writes, "You were born with potential. You were born with goodness and trust. You were born with greatness. You were born with wings. Learn to use them and fly."

If we want to take off in a new direction, we must first accept that we alone are responsible for all the good, the bad, and the ugly that manifests in our lives. Our lives unfold in equal measure to the thoughts we have and the choices we make.

We can no longer blame God, our parents, or the environment we grew up in for how our lives are unfolding. Can you imagine if the pilot of a plane you were on came out of the cockpit blindfolded and said, "I wonder where the plane is going to take us today?" Most of us navigate throughout our lives in the same manner, blindfolded and wondering where life will take us.

Life is rough. Life is tough. At times, life can undoubtedly suck.

ence? Siddhartha Gautama, The
t to find contentment, we must
You may have heard it said that
g on to this perception of life is

oolroom, my friends. We must
valk through life but learn and
given by William Ernest Henley
Invictus": "Out of the night that
to pole, I thank whatever gods
the fell clutch of circumstance,

I have not winced nor cried aloud. Under the bludgeoning of chance, my head is bloody but unbowed. Beyond this place of wrath and tears, looms but the horror of the shade, and yet the menace of the years finds and shall find me unafraid. It matters not how strait the gate, how charged with punishments the scroll, I am the master of my fate; I am the captain of my soul."

*I had* the privilege of sitting down and chatting with bestselling author Wayne Muller during a symposium sponsored by the Association for Global New Thought at the Unity Center in San Diego. In our discussion, I told Wayne one of my all-time favorite books is: *How Then, Shall We Live? I* have read, reread, studied, and practiced the principles outlined in this book for many years. In the book, Wayne asks us to consider four questions: Who am I? What do I love? How shall I live, knowing I will die? What Is my gift to the family of the earth?

My focus for this conversation was on Wayne's third question, how shall I live, knowing I will die? If you knew you had only a short time left here on planet earth and granted one final wish before you go, what would it be? At stake is nothing less than your legacy. Would you wish for more money, a better job, a new home, a more luxurious car? I hope the answer for all of us would be none of the above. When faced with death, one quickly realizes the only thing that matters in life is the relationships we have developed with others.

Before his untimely death from pancreatic cancer, Steve Jobs, the co-founder of Apple, said, "Remembering that I will be dead soon is the most important tool I've ever encountered to help me make the big choices in life. Because almost everything, all external expectations, pride, all fear of embarrassment or failure, these things fall away in the face of death, leaving what is truly important. Remembering that you are going to die is the best way I know to avoid the trap of thinking you have something to lose. There is no reason not to follow your heart."

I had the opportunity to ask myself this very question when diagnosed with lung cancer in 2011. One quickly learns how well he lived his life when confronted with death, not in the hypothetical, but when smacked right in the face with it. Dealing with life on life's terms can, at times, be extremely challenging. However, I could not think of one thing I'd left undone or felt the need to say during this experience.

To become proficient in any sport, the arts, medicine, or preparing a delicious meal, one must develop the discipline to practice their craft. One may ask, "How do I get to Carnegie Hall?" The answer is simple: "Practice, practice, practice." I am thankful throughout this entire ordeal; I did not feel any need to increase my prayer time or ask God for any special dispensation. I was all prayed up and ready to go.

Barring any reincarnation, we only live once, right? Wrong, we only die once. There is not a person on earth or a God in heaven that can change that reality for us. However, we can choose to be reborn several times a day if necessary. Comedian Billy Crystal put a positive spin on what he sees as stumbling blocks in finding the happiness we desire. Billy comments, "What's so fascinating and frustrating and great about life is that you are constantly starting over, all the time, and I love that."

Wikipedia defines inertia as "A property of matter by which it continues in its existing state of rest or uniform motion in a straight line unless an external force changes that state." We must break through the inertial pull of our resistance to change if we wish to keep moving forward. It is fear alone that keeps us from taking the necessary steps to break down our walls and forge a more meaningful life.

For some of us, even the mere thought of change can be terrifying. To prevent the uncertainty and fear inherent with transformation, we hang on to old, nonproductive clichés like, "if it's not broke, don't fix it," as a convenient way to cover up our hidden fears. Unless we understand how the principle of inertia works in our lives, we are doomed to repeat the same destructive behavior patterns.

Undoubtedly, we will have questions along the way. The answers to those questions will reveal themselves as we continue to move forward in our new direction. If we choose to do nothing, our path will be set in stone, sending us back onto the road of repetition. Jean Nidetch, the co-founder of Weight Watchers International, said, "It's choice, not chance, that determines your destiny." Choose wisely, my friends.

So why is it so hard for us to break through this wall of resistance? I believe it is an underlining feeling of unworthiness, a gift from our egos, perpetuating this nonsense. In her classic, *A Return to Love, Maryanne Williamson put forth," Our deepest fear is not that we are inadequate. Our deepest fear is that we are powerful beyond measure. It is our light, not our darkness, that most frightens us."*

R. Buckminster Fuller, speaking on unworthiness, said, "Never forget that you are one of a kind. Never forget that if there weren't any need for you, in all your uniqueness, to be on this earth, you wouldn't be here in the first place. And never forget, no matter how overwhelming life's challenges and problems seem to be, one person can make a difference in the world. It is always because of one person that all the changes that matter in the world come about."

Do you sometimes feel like a prisoner of your mind? Recycling thoughts of guilt, fear, resentment, and self-pity throughout the day? Believing you are not good enough? Not smart enough? Not rich enough? Are you praying God will finally hear your prayers and grant you a new partner, a chill place to live, a fancy car, or a better job? Until we stop trying to fill the void by accumulating things outside ourselves, we will never find that which we seek. You see, happiness is not lost; we are!

Each of us has the choice to either live creatively or self-destruct. External stimulation is not required to release the creative process. All we need is to awaken to the process, which is innate. Psychologists have long been telling us that we are only partially awake. That we, some more than others, only use a small part of our mental resources. We may appear to be alive physically but remain spiritually dead.

Researchers agree that about 10 percent of Americans over the age of twelve suffer from some manifestation of addiction. Unfortunately, that means about 90 percent of us still have our heads in the sand. You might be questioning, *What me? An addict? I don't drink, smoke, or do drugs of any kind.* As I have mentioned previously, addiction is not a chemical process. It is a spiritual void we try to fill with outside stimuli, which may bring temporary gratification but works in direct opposition to our long-term goals.

In *How to Live 365 Days a Year,* Dr. John Schindler writes: "Despite recent advances in medical research, the most widespread disease of all continues to rage unchecked, its name, emotionally induced illness. The number of its victims over 50 percent of all the sick in the United States. If every river in the nation were suddenly to flood, the damage would equal only a fraction of the amount this disease costs annually. In dollars and cents, in pain and human misery, emotionally induced illness constitutes humanity's single worst catastrophe."

I believe addiction is more prevalent today than in years past, primarily due to the preoccupation we have with the busy lives we lead. It is the crowding out of things that matter to that which is superficial and meaningless. We have become so attached to our "stuff" that we have lost sight of the things we say we value most. Dr. Michael Beckwith, a Unity friend and founder of the Agape International Spiritual Center, teaches, "Money has become our God and accumulation our practice."

Eckart Tolle writes in *The Power of Now,* "Not being able to stop thinking is a dreadful affliction, but we don't realize this because almost everyone is suffering from it, so it is considered normal. This incessant mental noise prevents you from finding that realm of inner stillness that is inseparable from being. It also creates a false mind-made self that cast a shadow of fear and suffering. Identification with your mind creates an opaque screen of concepts, labels, images, words, judgments, and definitions that block all true relationships."

Sigmund Freud theorized that most people do not want freedom because freedom involves responsibility, and most people are unwilling to take ownership of their lives. When we stare into broken mirrors, we see ourselves fragmented, alone, different, and apart. When we acknowledge, we are spiritual beings having a human experience; we can rise above our limitations. We will witness ordinary men and women, just like you and me, living extraordinary lives.

# 12

# SHEEP

WAR, FIRE, FAMINE, HURRICANES, TORNADOES, economic status, racism, illness, homelessness, and world politics are some of the reasons people cite for feeling spiritually disconnected. It is more likely we are praying to a power outside ourselves why most of us feel separated from their source. In addition to knowledge, one must be willing to take personal responsibility for the work involved in becoming a free thinker.

Most of us create our experiences not by tapping into our intuition but by surrendering our will and our lives over to a group of control freaks, keen on telling the rest of us how we are to think, feel, and act. We move through life as puppets on a string, going from one unconscious experience to another. Thus we have become a society of sheep, walking in circles, not having the courage to step out of the pack and forge an original path for ourselves.

Mark Twain quipped, "Sometimes I wonder whether the world is being run by smart people who are putting us on or by imbeciles who mean it." Out of fear of being labeled a nonconformist, we give the puppet masters permission to pull our strings and move us in the direction of their choosing.

I love the story of when government officials visited a tribe of Native Americans trying to explain the reason for daylight savings. During the meeting, one of the elders leaned over and whispered to his son, "Only the government would be so stupid as to cut a foot off the top of a blanket, sew it onto the bottom, and think they have a longer blanket."

Primo Michele Levi, a Holocaust survivor, wrote, "Monsters do exist in the real world, but they are too few to be truly dangerous in the long run. More dangerous are the common people with good intentions who are instantly ready to believe and act without asking questions." We must be more discerning in what information we accept as truth from unknown, unreliable, and unsubstantiated sources.

We all know that one special someone incapable of managing his or her own life but has an abundance of advice for anyone willing to listen. Leaving no stone unturned, our self-proclaimed saviors jump into any conversation by saying, "You know, I read somewhere," or, "They say with your condition, you should blah, blah, blah," as if the words came directly out of the mouth of God. Tweedy Bird put it this way, "In life, we must get things straight from the horse's mouth and not listen to the jackass spreading the gossip."

I recently received a greeting card with a picture of a young girl looking up at her mother. She asks, "Is it just me, or does everyone seem brainwashed, ignorant, and closed-minded yet still manage to offer an opinion on shit they know nothing about?" In this culture, it is difficult for our underdeveloped and overstimulated brains to process any creative thoughts of our own.

According to his official biography and still believed by most North Korean citizens today, Korean leader Kim Jong-il's birth took place on top of a sacred mountain. A new star was born on that day, and winter turned to spring. His biography also claims his body was "so well-calibrated" he never needed to defecate. Holy Moley, Batman, wouldn't that be cool?

Kim Il-sung, the first "Supreme Leader" of North Korea, told his citizens that sawdust was full of nutrients, encouraging them to chow down during their regular times of famine. I do not know about you guys, but I am sick and tired of choking on someone else's dust.

Were you troubled when I referred to us as a society of sheep? The word sheep is relatively inconsequential compared to some of the terms used to define our way of life by the rest of the world. One of my favorite TV personalities is the no-apology, tell-it-like-it-is host of HBO's *Real Time with Bill Maher*. Years ago, Bill received an unprecedented amount of criticism after referring to the people of America as "stupid." Although I am not comfortable using the word stupid to describe anyone but myself, I understand and support Bill Maher's sentiment.

News organizations have become not an inlet for the truth but an outlet for personal opinions, distortion, manipulation, and downright lies. I write this not as an indictment against our news organizations, whose business is to increase their market share, but for those of us who listen to and support this nonsense.

There is indisputable evidence of the saying "bad news sells." Fear has become the chief commodity sold to us by the mainstream media, who have progressively lost their way. Today, it is hard to find any substantial difference between supermarket tabloids and the mainstream media.

In years past, we heard reports that AIDS and Ebola may become worldwide pandemics, with the potential to eradicate every man and woman on the planet. Now, how often do you hear reports that with the current medication protocol, HIV can be rendered "undetectable" in the bloodstreams of those infected with the virus?

And how Ebola disappeared from the headlines when, in a few short months, our epidemiologists isolated the disease concentrated in West Africa, preventing its spread to other parts of the world. Today it is COVID-19 that has the world paralyzed in fear.

There was a time when reporters were men and women of integrity, like Walter Cronkite, trusted by everyone, who would say at the end of each broadcast, "And that's the way it is." Later in life, Cronkite would say, "I regret that, in our attempt to establish some standards, we didn't make them stick."

I felt honored when chosen to be part of the studio audience to film a companion video for Deepak Chopra's new book, *The Third Jesus*. The production set was two straight-back chairs on a small platform in the second-floor chapel at the Unity Center of San Diego. Wendy Craig-Purcell, the founding minister, was set to interview Dr. Chopra regarding his insights on *The Third Jesus*. Behind them, a beautiful water cascade enhancing the contemplative atmosphere in the room.

Before Wendy and Deepak took their seats on the platform, audience members entered the chapel to obtain our seat assignments. Next, they began filming, asking those of us in the audience to make facial expressions, such as smile, laugh, look amazed, be thoughtful, among others, which would be added later to the video for effect. There is nothing wrong or immoral about this practice. It is how filmmakers perform their craft, and if I wanted to be in the video, this was the price I paid for admission.

On an earlier occasion, an Orthopedic group asked me to put together an educational video for patients requesting additional, in-depth information about their upcoming surgeries. This production team brought with them a teleprompter, a piece of equipment I never heard of before. The producers said they would be uploading my talk onto the machine and control the speed at which I spoke during the filming.

When I finished writing my talk and presented it to management for their approval, the director of the center said he was, "Very impressed, and I should not change a thing." On the day of filming, however, I noticed they deleted one word from my original text.

In closing, I said something to the effect, "It is my hope and prayer you find this information valuable in helping you decide on any proposed surgical procedure you may be considering." Can you guess the one word they felt necessary to delete? Sadly enough, it was the word prayer.

Later, when discussing this issue with management, they explained they decided to take the word prayer out of my text, "So as not to offend anyone." Now, do you understand why I referred to us as a society of sheep? How is it that the word prayer has somehow become unacceptable for public consumption?

To help me navigate the many nuances of writing this book, I purchased one of the more sophisticated computer programs on the market. It corrected my spelling, punctuation, and grammatical errors and checked the world wide web for plagiarism. It also came with a politically correct monitor to keep me from using any inflammatory language.

Earlier, I outlined some professions our fathers worked in to provide a middle-class lifestyle for their families. I used titles like policemen, firemen, and garbage men in my descriptions, as these were the terms used for these positions by my parents' generation. In the 1950s and '60s, most women were not interested in these labor-intensive, "non-ladylike" jobs.

This program spits out gender-specific words; it does not consider "politically correct." I will always support women who stand up and fight for their rights to integrate into every aspect of society. However, the PC police must not have looked "down there" in recent memory. There are anatomic gender-specific differences between men and women that have stood the test of time. That is, of course, men have penises and women have vaginas.

The word penis has somehow eluded the politically correct war machine and is still called a penis. However, the always vulnerable vagina is once again under attack. "Va-jay-jay" has now become the word in vogue whenever discussing a woman's private parts. It is true, my friends, I heard it on Oprah! Out of respect for all women who have a vagina, I will no longer use that word in future writings.

I will, however, continue to focus my attention on the still politically correct, almighty penis.

Did you ever wonder why flowers and chocolate cost twice as much on Valentine's Day and Mother's Day as they did just a week prior? In the world of dollars and no sense, we get manipulated into purchasing merchandise we do not need and cannot afford. Advertisers guilt us into buying outrageously marked-up items to avoid being seen by our loved ones as cheap, unloving, self-centered jerks.

Although I will be staying far away from discussing any specific policies associated with our elected officials, left or right, it is easy to understand why Congress maintains such a low approval rating. As a medical professional having to deal with all the intricacies of health care, I was intrigued by the Affordable Care Act's passing into law.

After the bill was signed into law on March 23, 2009, Professor Johnathan Gruber, the chief architect of the ACA, was quoted as saying; "It was because of a lack of transparency and the stupidity of the American voter that helped Congress approve the Affordable Care Act." So maybe Bill Maher's comment about we Americans being "stupid" may not be so over the top after all.

Years ago, there were commercials on the radio for a company I thought was called Blow-Me. The first time I listened to this spot, I thought it was a comedy skit. In the commercial, I recognized a young, stereotypical California valley girl declare, Blow-Me can give you the cash you need without collateral, "because we trust you."

Claiming you can borrow $25,000 without collateral is one of the more perplexing business models I have ever encountered. As a businessman myself, I would like to offer you a once-in-a-lifetime opportunity. With me, you can borrow up to $1,000,000, no matter if you are unemployed, do not have any tangible assets, or wish to become part of the Taliban. If you are interested in our same-day cash delivery, please dial 1-(855) 42-Blow-Me.

When dealing with health, wealth, or the passing of a loved one, we become vulnerable to the carnies of the world selling snake oil from the back of a wagon. Even the field of medicine is not immune to this type of behavior. There are many great doctors out there who live by the credo *aeger primo* (the patient first). Some claim, however, to be compassionate physicians, but their primary interest is on the business side of medicine.

When my son was twelve, he had a pet guinea pig named Squealy. Before his fourth birthday, Squealy became severely dehydrated, no longer producing a viable amount of urine. One day, while examining patients in the clinic, I received a phone call from my wife, informing me she was at the vet's office with our children as Squealy appeared to be in a lot of pain. She said the vet took x-rays and found a calcified stone in his bladder, interfering with his ability to pee.

The vet was recommending major abdominal surgery. In the procedure, known as an ileal conduit, the patient's (human or bovine) ureters are surgically resected from the bladder and reattached to a piece of the intestine to direct urine through a stoma in the abdominal wall (an ileostomy) into an external collecting device.

Squealy would need to spend three days in the intensive care unit and would likely require post-op dialysis. The initial treatment would necessitate a payment up-front of $1,375. When asked by my wife what she should do, I told her to put the vet on the phone. Uh-oh!

When the vet picked up, I reiterated what my wife said and asked her if I understood the situation correctly. She acknowledged I did and added, "You have an extremely sick pig on your hands, Mr. Harrison. If we do not initiate treatment immediately, your pet pig will die." I rarely feel the need to inform a physician what I did for a living, but this was one of the times.

Now, I must say I loved Squealy, and if he had the slightest chance of surviving the procedure, I would have gladly paid for it. He reached the average lifespan of a guinea pig and could never make it through the recommended surgery. A young and healthy forty-pound dog might have a chance to survive, but not an emaciated geriatric guinea pig.

After the vet realized I knew what I was talking about, any sense this was an emergency quickly evaporated. In a sheepish voice, she asked what I would like for her to do. I told her to send Squealy back home with my wife and children, where, as a family, we would decide how best to help our little friend.

That evening, after the kids went to bed, I went into our backyard and dug a decent-sized hole behind some plants, knowing full well what I would be doing the following morning. I want to share the contents of a note I left behind for my son that day before heading off to work.

I wrote, "Hey, Jason, Squealy did not have a good night last night, and I would like your permission, if he is still in pain, to bring him back to the vet to stop his suffering." In the note my son left behind, he said, "Yes, Dad, you can take him to the vet. Tell Squealy I love him and know he's going to a better place. Bye."

That morning I contacted a different veterinarian who recently opened an office in our neighborhood. She invited me to bring the patient right in. After her examination, she told me our little friend was indeed dying, and she would be glad to help end his suffering. About ten minutes later, she came out from behind closed doors carrying Squealy in the same box he came in.

When she opened the lid, Squealy's head was placed on its side, lying on top of a small satin pillow shrouded in a linen blanket. I know it sounds nuts, but I would swear he was smiling at me. The vet handed me a sympathy card signed by the entire staff, along with his name and pawprint cast in plaster of Paris, and charged only a nominal fee to make Squealy's transition a peaceful one.

I hope I somehow contributed to an awareness of how savvy advertisers manipulate both the way we live and how we die. Like a used car salesman, funeral directors know they need to seal the deal in their first encounter with the family or risk losing their business altogether. They depend on our confused state of mind and the time constraints we are under to purchase one of their more expensive funeral packages.

When our mother passed, the funeral parlor's director first offered us their top of the line packages. As our entrepreneur of death explained, "I know your family wants only the very best for your mother." I wanted to tell this guy if my mother could find her way out of the refrigerator they put her in, she would read him the riot act for trying to pull such a con on her children. Our family chose to have our mother's body disposed of in the most simple, respectful, and dignified way possible. We opted for cremation.

We agreed on a reasonable rate for her cremation. According to state law, we needed to supply a container to place my mother's ashes before removing them from the premises. The funeral director pointed to some urns he had in stock priced well over a thousand dollars. When he saw the sticker shock on our faces, he quickly said, "Well, we do have a couple of outdated containers you can purchase for $500."

One urn distinguished itself from the others, and we believed Mother would have chosen this one for herself. The outside was hand-painted in pastels of purple, blue, and red with a hint of white. The pattern was reminiscent of Monet's *Water Lilies*, a painting that hung in my mother's living room for as long as I can remember.

The lesson I learned from these experiences is not to make impulsive decisions when under emotional distress. I have already purchased the container; my family will need to carry my little puff of dust out of the funeral parlor. My urn looks precisely like my mother's, but only cost six dollars and ninety-five cents at the local Goodwill. I have told my children I would like them to dump my ashes in the Hudson River near the Statue of Liberty, hoping to reunite with some of my old buddies playing pinochle at the bottom of the river.

# 13

# ANOTHER LOOK

A BORN-AGAIN CHRISTIAN WAS WALKING WITH A placard at a demonstration that read: "Warning to all whores, whoremongers, adulterers, adulteresses, porn-loving masturbators, sodomites, lesbian girlie men, manly women, immodest and rebellious women, alcohol drinkers, pot smokers, drug heads, tattoo getters, party animals, dirty dancers, potty-mouths, blasphemers, liars, gossipers, thieves, gangster rappers, rock and rollers, entertainment and sports worshipers, jewelry worshipers, parent haters, bitter people, merciless devils."

It goes on: "occult witches and sorcerers, money-hungry career pursuers, envious and thankless idolaters, prideful scoffers, God mockers Bible skeptics, atheists, evolutionist, pro-choices, two-faced church members, backsliders, Muslims, Buddhists, Hindus, Hare Krishnas, new-age gurus, Jehovah's Witnesses, Mormons, Christ-rejecting Jews, Mary-worshiping Catholics, sin-friendly heresy teachers, and every other form of life that is contrary to the holy law of God—hell awaits you if you do not abandon your sin and run to Christ for mercy."

I am sure we can all agree that throughout the ages, organized religion has not only caused friction between different faiths but Jew against Jew, Muslim against Muslim, and a variety of Christian sects against each other. I believe that organized religion has caused more harm than good, depressing more souls than it has ever resurrected.

In the book of Genesis 1:27 (ESV), we read, "God made man in His image and after His likeness." But man, driven by our self-centered foolishness, designs a god in our image and likeness. Is there any doubt why, as a society, we are so screwed up? This delusion of believing God thinks as we think is more prevalent and more destructive than all others combined.

"True believers" will hold on to their core beliefs come hell or high water. They will ignore, or try to rationalize, anything presented to them that does not support their core beliefs. According to Wikipedia, cognitive dissonance is the mental discomfort experienced by a person who simultaneously holds two or more contradictory beliefs, ideas, or values.

The faithful flock to churches, temples, and mosques to seek God, as if God is not available in restaurants, supermarkets, or sitting on a park bench. In most religions, one must use intermediaries; priests, rabbis, ministers, imams, gurus, and sages to intercede for us with God. However, a growing number of us would like to scream out with spiritual teacher Emmet Fox (1886–1951), "Why can't we have a firsthand and immediate experience with God?" The truth is, we can.

When asked if there was a hell, Pope Frances responded, "There is no hell; there is the disappearance of sinful souls." The pope's acknowledgment was in stark contrast to the two-thousand-year-old doctrine held by the Church. Their rebuttal came quickly. "The Church affirms the existence of hell and its eternity. Immediately after death, the souls of those who die in a state of mortal sin descend into hell, where they suffer the punishment of hell's eternal fire." I admire the courage demonstrated by Pope Francis when he said: "It is not necessary to believe in God to be a good person. In a way, that traditional notion of God is outdated. One can be spiritual but not religious. It is not necessary to go to church and give money. For many, nature can be a church. Some of the best people in history did not believe in God, while some of the worst deeds were done in his name."

I would like to understand better what Pope Frances meant by the "disappearance of sinful souls." But whatever he meant, it is light years ahead of the response from the Church. The pope said, "It is an honor to be called revolutionary." Doesn't Pope Francis remind you of a carpenter's son who lived some two thousand years ago and executed because he shared the same radical views that Pope Francis articulated so well?

I believe the living teachings of Jesus have been rendered sterile by religious zealots and dogmatic practices that leave us spiritually stagnating. In the past few decades, I have become somewhat desensitized by the sheer number of priests, ministers, and televangelists who talk a good game but lived by a different set of rules. Mahatma Gandhi quipped, "I like your Christ, but I do not like your Christians. Your Christians are so unlike your Christ."

An associate of mine and self-proclaimed born-again Christian posted a daily scripture passage on social media. One day he wrote, "Happy Columbus Day, the only white holiday we have left." I also had someone ask me during the Ferguson riots if I watched them "niggering around" on the news? They were caught off-guard by my reaction as I gasped, "Oh my God." The next words out of their mouth, were of course, "Not that I am racist or anything."

By the way, did the always amusing, cross-burning Ku Klux Klansmen ever come to realize that historically, Jesus was a dark-skinned Jew? He had parents not referred to as Mr. and Mrs. Christ? Scripture tells us Jesus regularly attended the temple (a Jewish church) and read from the Torah (the Jewish Bible). He was also known to share Passover meals and drink wine (Jewish Budweiser) with his other dark-skinned Jewish friends.

John Fugelsang was on point when he said, "Jesus was a radical, nonviolent revolutionary who hung around with lepers, hookers, and crooks. He was a long-haired, brown-skinned homeless, community organizing, anti-slut-shaming Middle Eastern Jew." So, let us join hands and burn another cross in Jesus's name. Going to church and reading the Bible does not make you any more Christian than walking into Starbucks will turn you into a Frappuccino.

Mark Twain quipped, "It is not those parts of the Bible; I can't understand that bothers me; it's the parts I do understand." I learned a valuable lesson one day while in the operating room, helping fix a broken hip on an elderly osteoporotic woman. There were five of us in the OR that day. Although we all came from different religious backgrounds, we all claimed Jesus to be our main way-shower.

Thank goodness this patient was anesthetized, for I broke one of the cardinal rules in operating room etiquette, discussing controversial topics (politics, religion, abortion, etc.) while in surgery.

I was quoting a well-known Bible passage when one of the nurses perked up and said, "It seems like you know a lot about the Bible, but there is something weird about you." She asked, "Do you take the Bible literally?"

I replied, "If you are asking if I believe God split the Red Sea, allowing Moses to escape the wrath of Pharaoh, I do not."

However, the way the story speaks to me is that the Jews found themselves spiritually blocked, wandering in the desert (our self-centered thinking) for forty years until God opened their hearts, which freed them from their self-imposed bondage.

The nurse grabbed me by the arm and said, "Oh my God, Sean, you're going to burn in hell."

When telling this story some ten years later, a member of our surgical team responded, "Well, that's just ridiculous. The only thing we need to believe is Jesus died for our sins and resurrected into heaven."

I am glad I learned something from my previous experience as I did not create any unnecessary cognitive dysfunction during this procedure.

As a kid, being raised Catholic was confusing in so many ways. As newborns, we begin our journey cursed with original sin, all because a woman took a bite out of an apple? There was not only heaven and hell but a mysterious third place called purgatory, where after we croak, our souls are put in storage until enough people pray on our behalf to receive a get-out-of-limbo-free card.

After first acknowledging we were not worthy of doing so, we ate Jesus's body and drank his blood. On Ash Wednesday, the priest drew a crucifix on our foreheads with what looked like finely ground charcoal, as he reminded us, "You were born from dust, and to dust, you shall return." And the Good News is?

When questioned if hell was real, a traveling minister replied, "Of course it's real. Have you not noticed the unusually high number of earthquakes and volcanoes we are experiencing lately? It is an indication that hell is so overpopulated, it is starting to break through the surface of the earth."

I brought my new bride, who was also raised Catholic, to our Saturday evening service to meet my "brothers and sisters" from a group I belonged to dedicated to the practice of first-century Christianity. During our communion service, we all stood in a circle as the priest broke the freshly baked unleavened bread, filling each of our hands with the now transformed "body of Christ." That evening, after acknowledging our presence with a nod of his head, the priest moved on. We stood in the circle with empty hands as everyone else participated in the sacrament.

A member of the group, who I will refer to as "Judas," informed the priest I was married before by the Church and never had that marriage annulled. The priest explained the Church could not recognize my current marriage as legitimate in God's eyes, but there was a way around it. I could go in front of a panel of six priests who will conclude (after paying $1,200) that my first marriage was never really a marriage in the first place. I passed on that offer but returned every Saturday evening and stood within the circle with empty hands for almost a year. In doing so, I felt more in communion with my brother Jesus than I ever felt before.

Most theologians agree that the earliest text incorporated into the Bible did not appear until 190 AD. The "Marcan Priority" that suggests Mark's Gospel came first continues to be held by most biblical scholars today. The Roman Emperor Constantine presided over the First Council of Nicaea, which convened from May 20 until June 19, 325 AD. Attended by most bishops of that time, this council was the first effort made by the Church to attain a consensus.

The council's main accomplishments were the settlement of God's divine nature, the Son, and his relationship to the Father, constructing the first part of the Nicene Creed, establishing uniform observance of Easter, and proclamation of early canon law. The Nicene Creed is still recited today by Catholics throughout the world during Sunday Mass. Although there are many versions to read from, this is how I remember it.

"We believe in one God, the Father almighty, Creator of heaven and earth, of all things seen and unseen. We believe in one Lord, Jesus Christ, the only Son of God. God from God, Light from Light, true God from true God. For our salvation, He came down from heaven and became man. He suffered, died, and buried. On the third day, He rose again and sits at the right hand of the Father. He will come again in glory to judge the living and the dead, and His kingdom will have no end."

I want to point out the First Council of Nicaea convened 325 years after the death of Jesus. Up to this point, there was no vote taken on the Trinity or the divinity of Jesus. No vote on the official biblical text. No consensus that Christianity would even be the official religion. In addition to Mark, Matthew, Luke, and John, the Gospels of Mary, Philip, and Thomas were considered but not voted in for inclusion.

Chinese whispers, also called "telephone" here in the states, is a favorite international children's game. Participants form a circle or a line. The first person whispers a phrase to the next, and so on until they reach the end of the line, where we get to hear the final version. The purpose of the game is to repeat the phrase without allowing it to become mangled along the way.

Part of the enjoyment in playing the game is seeing how convoluted the whisper ends up being. As well as being fun, this game has terrific educational value. It has been used in schools across the country to simulate the harmful effects of spreading gossip in our society. It shows how easily information can become misinterpreted and distorted in the lines of human communication.

The average lifespan of those living in the first century was approximately thirty-five years. This number held throughout the Dark Ages, the Middle Ages, and the Renaissance until the nineteenth century, when modern medicine began discovering its life-saving remedies. If my math is correct, which it probably is not, more than fifty generations have passed since Jesus walked the earth.

If your parents told you that one of your ancestors was born on top of a rainbow and never needed to pee or poo, what would you make of it? You would probably think this was a cool story, but place "Rainbow Man" in the same category as Santa Claus, Tinkerbell, and the Tooth Fairy. As we mature, these stories begin to unravel.

I feel the most cataclysmic decision ever made in man's entire history occurred after the First Council of Nicaea. There was a heretical movement known as Gnosticism, which believed knowledge rather than faith was the way to salvation. To stop its ever-growing popularity, the leaders of the Church voted Jesus in as very God. And yes, my friends, it was a vote and a close one at that.

Think for a minute if the vote had gone the other way and the council decreed Jesus was born in the same manner as you and I? What if they agreed that Jesus was not God taking human form but man becoming God? What if we had full confidence in one of the central teachings of Jesus: "All these things I have done, you will do, and greater works than these you will do"?

The Bible consists of hundreds of translations from one language, one culture, one idiom, and one generation to the next. Ask yourself this: Was Jesus a Christian? Did Jesus accept Jesus Christ as His savior? Jesus does not save, my friends; He inspires. It is only through His inspiration and our perspiration we are set free.

It would behoove us to reject the historical tendency to worship Jesus, the man. Jesus discovered and demonstrated God's loving nature to the fullest, which he said was within every one of us. He asked us to "Be perfect as your Father in heaven is perfect." Was Jesus putting us on, or did He believe we all have the same potential to do what He has done? If you identify yourself as a Christian and accept these words of Jesus to be Gospel, then as a community, we have to do better than this!

Charles Filmore, the cofounder of Unity, said, "What Jesus did we all could do, and it is fair to say that He is the normal standard for every individual. Every other expression of life is abnormal."

The Sufi poet Rumi cautions: "The spirit and the body carry different loads and required different attention. Too often, we put the saddlebags on Jesus and let the donkey run loose in the pasture."

Joseph Campbell writes: "The first floor of science is that the truth has not yet been found. The laws of science are working hypotheses. The scientist knows that at any moment, facts may be found that make the present theory obsolete."

The Dali Lama said, "If scientific analysis conclusively demonstrates certain claims in Buddhism to be false, then we must accept the findings of science and abandon those claims."

I believe the following story came out of *Reader's Digest* many years ago. It is about a young girl who did not want to go to bed when told to do so by her mother. The child said, "I don't want to sleep right now; I have some thinking to do." The understanding mother allowed her daughter to finish her thoughts before going off to bed.

The next morning the mother asked her daughter what it was she was thinking. The little girl said, "Well, Mommy, I was thinking about gravity and decided that gravity is God in the center of the world, keeping people right side up when the world is upside down." Maybe this is what Jesus meant when he said we must become open-minded like little children if we ever want to enter the kingdom of God.

Spirituality is not a one-day-a-week activity. All the books in the world will not help us if we do not practice what we have learned. We will be dealing with fundamental spiritual principles discovered and taught by Jesus and all the great mystics throughout the ages. Practicing these principles in our everyday life will empower anyone, addicted or not, to experience heaven right here and right now.

# 14

# SURRENDER OR NOT HERE I COME

I WANT TO BEGIN THIS CHAPTER BY PARAPHRASING one of my favorite animal stories, written by John Foster. It is about a pigheaded duck who could not surrender to its reality. See if you can identify with any or all of it.

> I am not a duck. I may look like a duck, walk like a duck, drink like a duck, and quack like a duck, but I am not a duck. I am an eagle in disguise. If you could prove it is respectable to be a duck, I might consider being one. But do not waste your time; I want to be an eagle.
>
> I think it is shameful to be a duck. It is so lonely here among all these ducks. But for some reason, none of the other eagles will have anything to do

with me. Why are eagles so cruel? Even if I were a duck, I would not stay a duck. I would become an eagle. I can be anything I want to be, and I want to be an eagle.

Ducks are terrible. I keep trying to swoop down and grab a rabbit, but I have webbed feet. Why would God make an eagle with webbed feet? If I starve to death, He will only have Himself to blame. The ducks all want to help, but what does a duck know about an eagle's problems?

Being an eagle is killing me. Not being a duck is killing me. I do not know what is killing me. Help me, dear God, help me. I am a duck; whether I like it or not, I am a duck. Ducks are some of the best people in the world. I love ducks. I am so incredibly grateful to be a duck.

Just like our feathered friend came to realize, not being who we are will tear at our souls until we surrender to what is. Owning our story can be frightening, but we must allow ourselves to become vulnerable. We must break through our most deep-seated fears to reach that elusive pot of inner peace at the end of the rainbow. Ralph Waldo Emerson said: "To be yourself in a world that is constantly trying to make you something else is the greatest accomplishment."

As I mentioned earlier, addiction is not a chemical process. No matter how it may manifest in our lives, this disease is rooted in feelings of low self-esteem and low self-worth, leading to an unconscious effort to self-destruct. The stories we tell ourselves and the decisions we make based on those stories are what make our lives unmanageable.

To negate these feelings, we search for outside stimuli to distract us from making peace with our reality. When our emotional pain level gets high enough, add a shot of heroin, a line of coke, a box of donuts, or a bottle of alcohol into the mix, and we are in deep trouble, my friends.

Surrendering to a power greater than ourselves, whatever name we give to it, is the only way I know to get out of our self-centered madness. We must resign ourselves that our old ways of thinking and living are no longer viable. By letting go of the past, we can co-create a new life by practicing the spiritual principles we associate with our higher self, love, kindness, compassion, empathy, honesty, open-mindedness, willingness, humility, integrity, joy, gratitude, and others. God's will for us then becomes our longing to allow the Creator to create in us all that is within itself.

When I started thinking about writing this kind of book, I asked family members if there were any standout memories during my active addiction. My sister (who found the suicide note I left when flipping out on acid) sent me this email. She asked, "Do you remember when I interviewed you to do a mental health assessment for one of my courses in grad school?"

The results showed I was borderline for antisocial personality disorder. However, being a sociopath was ruled out because of the high level of compassion I felt for others. She said, "You did some messed-up stuff but always had a good heart. Of course, the loud and clear diagnosis was a chemical dependency."

Before believing I had any redeeming qualities back then, I must remember this was the same sister who sneaked into an abandoned construction site with me to swing from a rope dangling from a crane. When it was my sister's turn to go, she positioned herself on the ten-foot platform my friends built for this purpose and held on for dear life. Her takeoff was picture perfect, but unfortunately, she forgot to let go of the rope for the last five feet of the ride and landed face-first into a concrete wall. She is also the same sister who, as a child, could not find her pacifier and picked up the pet turtle and sucked its head out of its shell. So, to my sister, whom I love dearly, you did some "messed-up stuff" yourself.

During my initial interview with my EPA counselor, he asked many questions about the relationship I had with my father. I started to get a little antsy with these questions and asked if I needed to talk about my father to get into the program? He said, "No, but I want you to understand the circumstances you found yourself in as a child were no fault of your own. It must have been terrifying for you to experience this type of behavior as a young boy."

I responded, "Nah, it wasn't that bad." When I left his office, I thought, *What the hell is wrong with me? How can that not have hurt?*

There is a story I love about a system used for capturing monkeys in the jungle. The goal is to take the monkeys unharmed for shipment to zoos across America. In this technique, the captors use heavy bottles with long narrow necks into which they deposit a handful of sweet-smelling nuts. The bottles are left on the jungle floor as the captors return to their base. Early the next morning, they return to find a monkey trapped next to each of the bottles.

The monkey, attracted by the smell, comes to investigate the bottle, sticks its arm down its long narrow neck, grabbing hold of the nuts. It cannot take its hand out of the bottle as long as it clings to the nuts but is unwilling to let them go. The bottle is too heavy to carry, so the monkey is trapped. We may laugh at the monkeys, but take another look because sometimes life makes monkeys out of us all.

If we want to let go of the past, we must accept what happened, happened; it is over, finished, done, so forget about it. It is time to turn the page. Our responsibility is to leave the past behind and reach forward to what the apostle Paul calls "The higher calling of God." We must be understanding and patient with ourselves throughout the process of our awakening.

Because it takes less time, effort, and stress to stay within our comfort zones, fundamental change will never come easy. Because we fear the unknown, surrendering to what is will be the most challenging part of our transformation. Here, we may find comfort in the words of Friedrich Nietzsche: "One must have chaos in oneself to be able to give birth to a dancing star."

Our ego's incessant rationalizations and denials make our path to surrender more complicated than it needs to be. If we cannot cut through the layers of bullshit we pile upon ourselves, any hope of recovery is stopped dead in its tracks. The ego is now in command. My mother, one of my real-life heroes, was also, without question, the queen of denial.

One day she returned early from work and burst into my room unannounced while I had a spike in my arm. I slammed the door shut and told her I would be right out. When I opened the door, she insisted I show her my arm. Since I only used the veins on my left side, I stuck out my right arm for her to see.

She seemed somewhat relieved and said, "Thank God, Sean. For a minute there, I thought you were using drugs."

During our family reunion in Mexico, one of my brothers was the only sibling out of the five still smoking cigarettes. While relaxing on a rainy night inside the villa, he quoted studies espousing the fact there were elements in tobacco that were good for your health. He is the same brother; however, when he was three years old insisted on drinking his morning coffee out of a baby bottle.

While reviewing patients' charts over my thirty-year career in orthopedics, I came across many stories that showed how deep one's denial could get. When putting together records for a medical/legal report, there was one H&P (history and physical examination) that I will never forget.

The subject's name and personal information are fictitious, protecting the innocent and complying with all HCFA regulations. Mr. Morass is a middle-aged male who presents to the emergency room complaining of irregular bowel movements after drinking heavily with friends a few days ago. He states he must have passed out, and "Somebody put a penny in my ass." The patient also reported several years ago having intercourse with men after a late night of partying. He is concerned but has been having regular bowel movements for the last couple of days. Jeez, I am still wondering about whatever happened to that penny!

For some, the need to recover may not originate from chemical dependency but from those experiences they had to endure growing up in a dysfunctional family. There are several twelve-step fellowships active today I believe can be helpful in these situations. The three that come to mind are Al-Anon, Nar-Anon, and ACOA (adult children of alcoholics). Alateen and Narateen are also available for those fortunate enough to find recovery early in life.

With permission, I am telling the story of a dear friend's real-life ordeal. Her story illustrates how some children can make it through the most horrendous circumstances without becoming chemically dependent. However, it does not mean they will not need to seek recovery at some point in their lives. No child goes through these types of experiences without being deeply scarred. I believe it is here where addiction takes root.

Kimberly, now in her mid-forties, her marriage ending in divorce after twenty-four years, shared her story: "I never knew I was born into such a dysfunctional family. By the time I was ten, it had become evident my dad had a drinking problem."

Growing up, Kim loved watching professional hockey on television. A few months before her parents separated, she begged her dad to take her to a game. He did so, but reluctantly. When they got to their seats in the arena, Kim sat alone throughout the entire game. When the game finally ended, she found her dad sitting at the bar with some friends, and they headed home.

On the way back, she said he was driving erratically, swerving in and out of traffic. He accused her of wanting to go to the game only to spy on him for her mother. "This night was one of the few times I ever heard my parents argue," she said. Typically, they never raised their voices.

Sometime in the mid-1980s, Kim said her dad started drinking heavily and appeared more depressed than usual. One day he lost all control. Kim remembers being alone in the apartment she shared with her mom and younger sister studying for her eighth-grade finals. She received a call from her mother's friend, informing her that her mother had been shot and taken to the hospital.

As she anxiously waited outside the house for her mother's friend to pick her up, a police cruiser rolled up the driveway. The officer said she was being placed in protective custody and needed to go with him. On their way to the station, a call came over the radio, asserting the man suspected in her mother's shooting was in custody, and that man was none other than her father.

"I was terrified," she said.

When they got to the station, the officer took her into a large room and sat her down. He said, "I need to tell you something, and you must be strong." He explained after her father shot her mother, he went to the home of her maternal grandparents', shooting them both to death. That evening Kim's four-year-old sister was in the house where the shooting took place. She hid behind the living room couch as her father began to fire.

When the carnage was over, her sister ran out of the house, telling her neighbors, "Grandma and Grandpa are dead." Both were lying on the kitchen floor, mortally wounded. "Blood was everywhere," she said.

Now a convicted murderer, her father said he wished he never took a sip of alcohol that night. He spent the rest of his life in prison and died alone in his cell.

Kimberly said, "Thirty-five years after the shooting, I can see how growing up in this environment has affected me throughout my life, especially in my close, intimate relationships with others. I never learned how to communicate my deep feelings of hurt with anyone."

Melissa, a friend who entered recovery by the time she was twenty, tells her story this way. "I cannot remember a time in my life when I loved myself." Melissa's mother and father were Jewish, who never married and split up when she was three. She lived with her mother, who remarried a non-Jew, always a contentious point in their marriage. They had two children together. "I felt like a tagalong in my mother's new family," she said.

Although her mother was not chemically dependent, she was disconnected and showed no interest in Melissa whatsoever. Melissa followed the Jewish tradition until the age of nine, when she realized she no longer wanted religion to be part of her life, which was intolerable to her mother. Melissa was shipped off to live with her father.

Unfortunately, her father was an addicted, mentally ill pedophiliac gambler, who, unlike her mother, gave her plenty of attention. Melissa said, "He made me feel beautiful by telling me how sexy my body was. He made sure I was always looking good for the boys. When I lost weight, he shamed me because my breasts became smaller and no longer attractive."

Although her father never physically assaulted her, he often questioned her about her intimate experiences with boys. "He was quite proud when I told him I gave a boy head for the first time. I equated my father's love with how many sexual partners I had. He attached such pride in my promiscuity. I felt the only way I could gain acceptance from him was to sleep with as many boys as possible."

Eventually, all the drugs in the world, including heroin, could no longer silence the voices in her head. Melissa recalls the first time she took apart a razor and started to cut. She said, "I would carve the word fat into my upper thigh, so every time I used the restroom, I could remind myself how worthless I was." She quickly learned by cutting; she could override some of the emotional pain she experienced by creating a more intense physical pain. So cutting became her new addiction.

At eighteen, right after high school, she found herself institutionalized due to chemical dependency and depression with suicidal ideation. She would say her favorite fantasy was lying on railroad tracks playing chicken with an approaching train. One month later, she checked herself into rehab.

I first met Melissa, who was barely twenty-one when she introduced herself on a night I spoke at a coffee shop in downtown San Diego. It was apparent she was serious about her recovery and was willing to go to any lengths to obtain it. She said she was doing well regarding her addiction to drugs and coping with bulimia, but she was still cutting herself to ease her emotional pain.

One year later, I heard Melissa speak at a meeting and was amazed by how much she grew since the last time we spoke. In a private conversation, she showed me her arms and said, "Look, I stopped cutting myself." But before I could get the word congratulations out of my mouth, she said, "However, I began burning myself instead."

And tomorrow, my friends, we all begin anew.

According to Roman history, the people of Rome carried a white stone as proof of their citizenship. This stone meant they had the full power of the Empire behind them. If a Roman citizen was ever convicted of a crime and sent to prison, the stone was taken away and given back only when they completed their sentence.

Today, the stone remains a symbol that we can wipe the slate clean and step beyond our self-imposed prison walls. For us, the stone represents the hope of things to come. We have served our sentences, my friends, and are now free to live the kind of lives we desire—not by chance but by choice.

# 15

# BROTHER CAN YOU SPARE
# A LITTLE CHANGE

USED BY MINISTERS AND CHURCH GROUPS throughout the 1930s and 40s, the Serenity Prayer— "God, grant me the serenity to accept the things I cannot change, the courage to change the things I can, and the wisdom to know the difference"—is one of the most recognized prayers throughout the world. Its simplicity and practicality transcend all languages, cultures, and religious beliefs. It lays out a set of principles that, in and of themselves, can dramatically change our lives for the better.

Think about how much time, effort, and emotional turmoil we put into trying to unhappen the things happening all around us. We try to unhappen the weather, the morning news, the way we look in a mirror, and the fact we need to get up at five o'clock to go to a job we do not like. Above all, we try to unhappen the opinions others may or may not have about us. As sure as the principle of mathematics dictates 2+2=4, when we try to unhappen that which is, unhappiness and frustration are sure to follow.

There is great wisdom in the ancient Chinese saying, "When the winds of change blow, some people build walls while others build windmills." I still have a button on my rock and roll jacket from the 1970s that says, "Everything in the universe is subject to change, and everything is on schedule." Change can be challenging, but nothing is more demoralizing to the human spirit than being stuck in a self-imposed prison of our past. Life is not a playground but a schoolroom, where the winds of change can become our best teachers.

Are you fearful, guilt-ridden, judgmental, self-righteous, resentful, irresponsible, jealous, prideful, arrogant, dishonest, controlling, rigid, manipulative, demanding, closed-minded, overly dramatic, insensitive, disconnected, materialistic, grandiose, paranoid, defensive, over-analytical, a gossiper, rebellious, lustful, abusive, greedy, critical, sarcastic, intolerant, lazy, vengeful, inconsiderate, dishonorable, or codependent?

These are the roots of addiction that separate us from the love of God and our fellow man, compelling us to search for things outside ourselves to bridge this illusion of separation. These personality traits lay the groundwork for developing a chemical dependency or activating any number of process addictions, including shopping, gambling, overeating, hoarding, pornography, and excessive internet socialization.

A parable from the Cherokee tradition tells a story of a father speaking to his curious son. The father said, "My son, there is a battle between two wolves inside us all. One is evil. It is angry, frightened, jealous, greedy, resentful, dishonest, and desperate. The other is good. It is joyful, peaceful, loving, humble, compassionate, kind, empathetic, and truthful." The son thought for a moment and then asked his father, "Which wolf wins?" The father replied, "The one you feed, my son."

This parable illustrates how the twelve steps work for anyone willing to participate in the process. Slowly but surely, with the help of those who walked this path before us, we can learn how to minimize addiction's devastating effects by feeding the loving side of our nature. It is by practicing these spiritual principles we can keep this patient, insatiable killing machine in remission.

I like to use the analogy of overcoming addiction by chopping down a mighty oak. The leaves and branches of the tree represent our obsessive/compulsive thinking. Our compulsion to act emanates directly from our obsessions and is the primary cause of our lives becoming unmanageable. The tree's roots represent our inner state of consciousness described by many as infantile self-centeredness.

The ego of the addicted mind will trick us into believing significant harm or even death will occur if we do not act upon our obsessive thoughts. When we begin to rely on outside stimuli to make our insides feel better, it will not be easy to stop. If you want to kill a tree, you would not be successful by picking off some of its leaves or by sawing through its branches. We must dig deep and sever the roots that feed the entire tree.

In a five-part PBS series on the Neuroscience of Addiction, Dr. Timothy Fong, an addiction psychiatrist, explains, "I tend to think of addictive disorders as a general umbrella term for all sets of behaviors that refer to repetitively taking or doing something despite harmful consequences. Whereas when we use the term addiction, I think that should mean to say my set of behaviors is causing me significant harm, but I keep doing it despite the harm that it brings."

Susan Ferguson, Ph.D. from the department of psychiatry and behavior at the University of Washington, said, "Addicts continue using these maladapted behaviors we see with addiction. So not only would drug addicts have more of an urge to take drugs, but the parts of the brain that would normally tell you that is not a very good idea; those parts become dysfunctional and kind of go away. So not only do they have a stronger urge to take drugs, they don't have anything telling them that's a bad idea."

Dr. Keith Witt, a licensed psychotherapist who treats clients with chemical addictions and behavioral or process addictions, explains, "Addiction makes you more prone to addiction. To somebody who is an alcoholic, they are more likely to be addicted to gambling. Someone who is a sex addict is more likely to have problems with drugs and alcohol, and they are more likely to develop these problems in recovery, even after many years of abstinence."

It is courage alone that stands between our fears and any spiritual awakening we may experience. If we wish to remain under the ego's direction, the same lessons we should have learned years ago will reappear. They will remain part of our lives until we find the strength to let go of our narcissistic tendencies. If we can pause for just a moment and see through the illusions created by the ego, we will find within ourselves all the courage needed to release our past and begin anew.

The Buddha taught, "When the student is ready, the teacher appears."

In future chapters, I will discuss what I believe are the four most spiritually stagnating emotions we experience as human beings: fear, guilt, resentment, and self-pity. These are the four pillars of addiction that prop up and justify our addictive patterns of behavior.

Years ago, I co-facilitated several adult discussion groups at one of the many great spiritual communities in San Diego. At one of our meetings, we discussed the concept of letting go by utilizing this principle, "You may not be able to stop the birds from flying overhead, but you can prevent them from building nests in your hair." It matters not what happens to us or around us; the only thing that truly matters in life is what happens within us.

There is no getting around it; unfortunate things happen in life, and there are many reasons one may find themselves a little blue from time to time. Some have lost jobs, spouses, homes, experienced bankruptcy, suffered a catastrophic illness, or endured the untimely death of a loved one. Others may have experienced the cruelty of addiction or the physical, mental, or sexual abuse by another.

Typical is the cry, "Why did this happen to me?" We must

remember, addiction is a family disease, and sickness begets sickness. If we admit we are powerless over our addiction, we must also recognize that we have no power over others' addictive behaviors. We do not get sucked into addiction by some mysterious genetic process or by the luck of the draw. It is through our living experiences and our inability to cope with those experiences that seals our fate.

I believe it happens something like this. Mommy meets Daddy, they have a few drinks together, and after huffing and puffing in the back of Daddy's car for a minute or so, Daddy moans, and Mommy gets mad. Nine months later, we slide out of our little secure baby caves and land in a world of absurdity. It is in this psychosocial atmosphere where I believe we become indoctrinated into the world of addiction.

Before I share my thoughts on the innate power we all possess to overcome our challenges, I want first to acknowledge that many of us who are addicted also suffer from clinical depression. All my siblings have been on antidepressant medications at some point in their lives. We may ask the question, which came first, the chicken or the egg? Does one develop depression because of an addiction, or does depression cause the addict to self-medicate?

Like an addiction, depression is indiscriminate and can strike anyone at any time. Those who meet the criteria for a major depressive disorder find themselves withdrawing from society and everyday activities. Even the thought of brushing our teeth can be overwhelming. In my experience, depression is not merely an absence of happiness but a belief we will never experience it again.

In my early fifties, a dark cloud fell upon me that felt more physical than psychological. It was hard for me to do anything except try to get through another day. While driving on the highway, I would scan places where it would be impossible for me to survive if my car were ever to "accidentally" swerve off the road.

I went to see my doctor and told him it was my medical opinion that I was suffering from liver failure, most likely a byproduct of my many years of active addiction. He said he would take the appropriate tests but believed I was suffering from a major depressive episode. It turned out my liver function tests were completely normal. He placed me on a common antidepressant, and after a few weeks, I started to feel myself again.

Today, most patients respond exceptionally well to treatment, which may include both medication and therapy. When addiction and depression are intertwined, we will need all the help we can get, medicine, psychology, spirituality, and, most importantly, a support group. These are lifelong processes that have no cure. If you or someone you love shows signs of clinical depression, put this book down and get help right away. Untreated depression is as deadly as injecting a hot shot of heroin.

# 16

# FEAR AND FAIRY TALES

D ID YOU EVER WAKE UP AND, FOR NO APPARENT
reason, feel uneasy about the day ahead? Your life circumstances
appear virtually the same as yesterday, but somehow today, you feel
discouraged and overwhelmed. When we experience generalized
anxiety like this, psychologists will tell us we are experiencing a
biophysical reaction to our perception of reality, not reality itself.

Most spiritually aware people understand that fear is not what
we see but how we perceive. As an acronym, FEAR is false evidence
appearing real. By the time we reach adulthood, some of us have
become so accustomed to meet the unknown from a fear-based
perspective; it becomes just another bad habit.

It is not the darkness we are afraid of but the boogiemen we
place within it that causes our fear. We are not afraid to love but
fear the hurt we experience when our love gets rejected. We are not
frightened of heights but of the ramifications of falling.

For example, say you were walking through the forest, and along the way, you encountered a fast-running stream you needed to cross. Someone was kind enough to lay down a thick wooden plank to serve as a bridge spanning three feet above the water. Would you cross it? I believe most of us would. Now suppose the plank was six feet high. The structure itself has not changed, but somehow we shifted our focus from the sturdy plank beneath our feet to what would happen if we slipped and fell.

I have heard it said, "Worrying is like sitting in a rocking chair. It gives us something to do, but it doesn't get us anywhere." Are you one who never attempts anything new because you fear failing or being judged by others? Are you reluctant to meet new people because you fear their rejection? We may be afraid of doctors, not because we are sick, but because they might find something we did not know previously existed.

Fear is essential for our survival, protecting us from the onslaught of perceived dangers we encounter throughout our day. Our fear becomes neurotic, however, when common everyday concerns morph into phobias. We may intuitively know our high level of anxiety is not rational, but we stand incapable of doing anything about it. Unfortunately, those addicted are exponentially more likely to suffer from the paralyzing effects of fear than those who are not.

What would you think is the most pervasive fear we face in our society today? Would it be the fear of flying? Fear of heights? Fear of the dark? Fear of fire? Fear of spiders and snakes? Fear of intimacy? Fear of illness or death? There is nothing too trivial to provide a threat to someone who has become a compulsive worrier.

Strangely enough, the most prolific fear we experience is of public speaking, which I believe is triggered by a subconscious fear of not being appreciated or being labeled a fraud. More than 70 percent of the US population think their careers have suffered due to their self-centered fear of public speaking.

Some of our fears are entirely rational, like when children touch a hot stove; they quickly learn never to do that again. Or like me, when you stand on the top rung of a ladder where it advises "*Do not stand,*"

and as you are falling, realize there is no "gravity god" going to save you from all the hurt you are about to experience. These are healthy fears. However, once the ego gets involved, it rapidly turns molehills into mountains. The most trivial challenges can turn into life and death scenarios, overriding all rational thoughts and feelings.

Many will cry out, "But if you were in my shoes, you'd be worried too." It was Nelson Mandela who said, "I learned that courage was not the absence of fear, but the triumph over it. The brave man is not he who does not feel afraid, but he who conquers that fear." The best way to lessen the effects of deep-seated fears is to introduce the individual to the very thing they fear incrementally. In the same way, one would receive treatments to alleviate the effects of seasonal allergies.

We must remember, all thoughts are formative. We will be discussing the power of our minds throughout the remainder of this book. Marcus Aurelius, the wise Roman emperor in the second century, understood the nature of our fears when he said, "Let others pray not to lose their children, let me pray not to fear to lose them." He added, "It is not death a man should fear, but he should fear never beginning to live."

According to Kathy HoganBruen, Ph.D., spokesperson for the National Mental Health Association, "While we don't know exactly why or where phobias originate, they are a type of mental illness, with genetics as well as the environment playing a role, meaning maybe someone had a negative or traumatic experience related to the core of their phobia."

With all due respect to Dr. HoganBruen, I disagree with the premise that "maybe" phobias are related to adverse or traumatic events. In my experience, I believe that most phobias can trace back to a specific incident or repetitive trauma.

One of the more apparent fears I faced as a child, which has gently followed me into adulthood, is the oh-so-common fear of going to the dentist. Throughout grade school, we "poor kids" were bused from Queens into Manhattan and brought to one of the most prominent dental schools of its time, and if it was not for them, I doubt I would have a single tooth left in my mouth.

Many patients labeled this clinic as the primary source of their paralyzingly fear of the dentist. Some say it was a place where they could imagine Stephen King shooting his next horror film. As soon as I heard my name called over the school's loudspeaker to line up for the bus ride into Manhattan, I would start to panic.

The building itself was a massive six-story brick structure that looked more like a warehouse than a dental clinic. Each floor contained row after row of identical dental stations separated by a thin white translucent curtain. Every aspect of being in the clinic, from the bleach-like smell that permeated the building to the drills' constant high-pitched shrieking, elevated my fear to a fever pitch. Although I still get anxious about going to the dentist, I am happy to report it has not become a long-term phobia.

One of my sisters owned a ground-level condominium in Bonita Springs, Florida. This area is known not only for its beautiful beaches but also for its vast array of natural habitats for various critters, including the alligator, who still reigns supreme. Florida has a million-plus of these prehistoric killing machines lurking in its lakes, lagoons, swimming pools, and golf courses. Few members of the animal kingdom have survived the evolutionary process longer than the alligator. They are cold-blooded creatures often found basking in the sun to recharge their batteries.

When our kids were still in grade school, we would plan family vacations during spring break somewhere in the tropics to spend some quality time together. One year we booked an exciting trip to the Hawaiian island of Kauai, which included a helicopter ride over an active volcano and sailing up and down the beautiful Na Pali Coast.

In the week before we were to leave San Diego, Kauai was deluged with torrential rains that shut down many of its roads, forced hotels to close, and disrupted much of the air traffic over the Hawaiian

Islands. The question was where we could book a trip a day or so before spring break began without paying an arm and a leg to do so.

My sister offered us her condo for the week. Our children's primary interest was to ride on a flatboat exploring the Everglades. Mine was to read a couple of good books while sipping freshly squeezed orange juice and fish from dawn to dusk from the back porch of my sister's condo. The lagoons weaving in and out of this community were relatively shallow, making it a prime location for largemouth bass, and I could not wait to get out there.

Since this was the first time staying at my sister's place in Florida, she briefed us about all the little nuances we needed to know. She told us where to pick up the key, where to eat, and, most importantly, where her husband kept his fishing poles.

She cautioned us about an adult alligator that basked in the sun in the back of her property. She also said a bobcat recently came up to their back door looking to sink its teeth into the neck of her bitesize chihuahua.

Before leaving San Diego, I made an error in judgment by searching the internet for stories involving man's encounters with alligators while fishing. I watched a man reeling in a decent-sized bass when an alligator grabbed hold of it just a few feet from shore. Not wanting to lose the fish, the angler continued to fight the gator. This error in judgment cost him a chunk out of his lower leg.

The landscape around my sister's condo was a carbon copy of what I saw in the video.

I set my alarm for 5:30 the next morning to make sure I got out there at sunrise when the fish are most active. I was hoping to land a three-pounder to have for dinner that evening but unfortunately fell somewhat short of my goal.

After lunch, I went back out with rod in hand, and for the first time laid eyes on the behemoth; my sister warned us about lying in the sun on the other side of the lagoon. I felt both exhilarated and intimidated by being in the presence of this mysterious beast that lurks in the shadows.

I walked the length of the lagoon, casting my line around dead trees and bushes, where bass like to congregate. At the end of the development was a chain-link fence separating the waterway from the rest of civilization. Feeling a little uneasy, I turned to take my line out of the water when I noticed a smaller five-foot gator standing high on all fours, staring me down. It stayed at the water's edge with its mouth open, waiting for a free meal, which I did not have, nor would I have given.

I walked back toward the safety of my sister's condo when I noticed my new reptilian friend following me along the banks. I also noticed that our resident master-gator was no longer visible. With its batteries now fully charged, he must be out searching for an early evening snack. I concluded I was on the menu that evening. I felt an intelligent, well-coordinated effort, just like the raptors used in Jurassic Park, to box me in and drag me into the water.

The smaller gator followed me back to the condo, and just as quickly as it appeared, it slithered back into the darkened water. I never did see the larger of the two gators again. I continued to fish that week, but only at sunrise, armed with a thick bamboo baton. I am happy to report my fear of alligators was situational, never developing into an adult phobia.

As a teenager, I often traveled into Manhattan to visit our furry friends at the Central Park Zoo. I usually brought along a large bag of peanuts and fruit to feed the elephants, primates, and the many squirrels gathering nuts for the winter. My modus operandi was to hop the four-foot perimeter fence and hand-deliver a piece of fruit to my all-time favorite primate, the magnificent silverback gorilla.

It was all good until one day, when the gorilla reached between the bars and snatched the entire bag of treats, along with my arm, smashing me against the steel bars of his cage. Although I often thought about it, "something" must have been looking out for me, as I never did bring raw meat to feed the lions, tigers, and bears, oh my.

Even when I am astutely aware my fear is unwarranted, it still could override any rational thoughts I may have had. For many years my friend Daniel, a fine Scottish lad, and I cosponsored the youth program at a universal spiritual community center in San Diego. Once on a beautiful summer's day, we took the teenagers to La Jolla Shores to have a family fun day at the beach. Along with their role as chaperones, the students' parents stepped up big time, bringing lots of food, drinks, and various beach games. We also had access to a pair of kayaks to use throughout the day. Daniel braved the surf several times, taking along some of the students who had never kayaked before. On one of his outings, just a few hundred feet offshore, Dan came across a school of black-tipped sharks.

While vacationing in Tahiti, I had the opportunity to dive alongside these fast-moving eating machines crisscrossing the frozen carcass of a billfish the crew threw overboard twenty minutes before we hit the water. It is well known these sharks rarely attack people unless provoked. When we made it to the area, Daniel stood up to look for the sharks, but in doing so, he tipped the kayak, and we both hit the water.

As we were airborne, Daniel accidentally smacked me on the left side of my head with his paddle, slicing through my outer ear. In my mind, as I saw my blood dripping in the water, those docile blacktip sharks instantly turned into man-eating great whites.

I panicked and swam as fast as I could to get back to solid ground. A couple of stitches later, I was as good as new. I am happy to report my encounters with the sharks have not turned into an ongoing phobia.

After high school, I was one of six students accepted into a two-year x-ray technician program at a well-known cancer hospital on the east side of Manhattan. During one of our rotations, my senior partner and I would take a portable x-ray machine along with us to shoot studies throughout the hospital. These portables were for those patients not capable of making it down to the x-ray department.

One afternoon we got called to the triage area to obtain a chest x-ray of an emaciated woman who appeared to be in her late eighties. The patient had a tracheostomy performed earlier in the day. This new study was to rule out pneumonia. As students, we were unsure if the patient was dead or alive, but we needed to shoot the X-ray in any event.

Our first order of business was to place a thick metal cassette under the patient's back without causing injury. As my partner began the count— "one, two, three"—I got as close to the patient as possible, grabbing hold of the sheet beneath her, and lifted. As I did so, the patient coughed, and the most disgusting ball of yellowish-green gunk I have ever seen in my life came shooting out of her neck.

It hit me on the right side of my forehead, and as I was pulling away, it draped over my right eye, across the bridge of my nose, and wrapped around my lips. It took years before I could tell this story without gagging. I have never shied away from cleaning a patient's pee, poop, or vomit throughout my career. However, getting hit with another phlegm ball remains a phobia of mine that I have never been able to shake.

# 17

# CABEZA CON ANGER BANGER

MERRIAM WEBSTER DEFINES ANGER AS "A STRONG feeling of displeasure and usually of antagonism." Anger is a self-defense mechanism that surfaces when someone acts in a way we perceive as threatening or disrespectful. For the non-addict, anger is a valid emotion that often leads to dialog and conflict resolution. It only becomes a problem when our egos get involved making us do or say things; that are not in our best interest.

When angry impulses are unresolved at the time of a perceived injury, anger turns into resentments, flatlining the souls of the addicted and non-addicted alike. Unlike anger, which is usually spontaneous and fleeting, holding on to our grievances is a choice we make. One of the Founding Fathers of our Constitution, Benjamin Franklin (also the face on the $100 bill), quipped, "Anger is never without reason, but seldom a good one."

None of us can receive the universe's invitation to love when we continue to recycle all the hurts; we alone planted in our consciousness in the first place. Holding onto resentments will not change the circumstances or cause any discomfort to the person we resent. Most of the time, we direct our resentment toward a person who usually has no idea we are harboring such feelings about them. We bottle our anger and play the role of victim to justify our self-righteousness.

We must learn that forgiveness is not something we do for the person we resent but in and for ourselves. When we forgive, we are not excusing others' bad behavior but are deciding we will no longer let these feelings control our lives. The Buddha taught that holding onto anger is "like drinking poison and hoping the other person will die."

How can we co-create a better life for ourselves when we believe everything that goes wrong in our lives is someone else's fault? When my resentments rise to the surface, I find it helpful to ask myself, would I rather be right, or do I want to be happy? To forgive or not to forgive, this is the question. It is also a choice we alone will make.

These are some of my personal experiences dealing with anger, which has dogged me throughout my recovery. Like the characters Dr. Jekyll and Mr. Hyde, created by Robert Louis Stevenson in 1886, I can switch from being a monk to a madman in the blink of an eye. I am somewhat embarrassed to say all these incidences occurred after I was drug-free for more than a decade.

I knew I needed to do something about my anger issues while working in an Orthopedic Hospital in New York City. One day, the usual twenty-minute train ride from Queens into Manhattan took more than an hour. My routine was to get to work thirty minutes early, chow down on a freshly baked muffin, sip on black coffee, and plan out my day. This day I arrived with only minutes to spare.

I put my coffee and muffin on a table in the nurse's lounge and ran to the locker room to change into my scrubs. When I returned a few minutes later, my coffee was still on the table, but my muffin was gone. I do not know if it was the frustration from the extra-long train ride into the city that triggered my madness, but I lost it. I ran around kicking doors open and screaming, "Who took my muffin?"

As I was scrubbing my hands, a young man whose job it was to clean the operating rooms between procedures came up to me and said, "I am sorry, Sean. I ate your muffin. I was very hungry." Our housekeeping crew worked extremely hard for little compensation, and my twenty-two-year-old muffin thief just had his first child. That day I earned a new nickname from my peers in the Operating Room: "The Click."

I was in my office at home, dictating medical reports when I heard a loud knock on the door. Our visitor was a young man selling high-quality meats from the back of his truck. My wife was quick to reach the door and gave her usual warm greeting. I could not understand a word this young man was speaking, but I kept hearing my wife say, "No, thank you, we are not interested."

After the third time, I jumped out of my chair and raced to the door, screaming, "Did you not hear what she said? We are not interested in buying your stupid meat," and demanded he gets off my property as I slammed the door in his face.

When I turned around, my wife was in the kitchen, sobbing. When I asked what was wrong, she replied, "Sean, that man was deaf."

I spent an hour that day searching the neighborhood for this young man's truck to apologize for my behavior and purchase all the meat he had left to sell. I was never able to find him that day or since. Twenty years later, this story still makes me cringe every time I think about it.

One day, as I was driving from one clinic to another in light midday traffic, I got off the highway as I usually do, staying in the left lane to make a left turn at the light. I noticed a car from two lanes over trying to maneuver its way in front of me. As soon as I realized what he was trying to do, I stopped to let him in, but unfortunately not quick enough.

He got stuck at the light with one car in front of him and me behind. I saw him slam his fist on the dashboard. He looked directly at me through his rearview mirror and mouthed the words, "You f@#+ng a-hole."

It was like I rehearsed this scenario a thousand times. I put my car in park, got out, and took off my shoes. In Tae Kwon Do, we always train barefoot. Once my shoes are off, I am all in; there is no turning back.

The driver saw me walking up to the car and rolled down his window. The first thing he said was, "Don't you know who I am?"

I replied, "Yes, I do know who you are. You're the guy who just called me an a-hole. Now get out of the car."

Fortunately for both of us, the light turned green, and he went from zero to sixty in three seconds. I stood there at the intersection without shoes, wearing dress pants, a white shirt, and a tie, topped off by my lab coat, just in time for my afternoon clinic.

In a separate road rage incident that very well could have ended my life on a highway, I got off early from work on a picture-perfect day here in San Diego. I was driving in the right-hand lane, doing about sixty-five mph, which is the speed limit. I felt incredibly grateful for the comfortable life our family has enjoyed here in America's Finest City.

As I approached Aero Drive, the right lane became an exit only, so I put on my blinker, looked in the mirror, and slowly inched over to the left. A car not visible seconds before came up fast, wanting me to abandon my lane change to get off at the exit. As I did not feel safe moving back to the right, the driver was forced to get into the lane behind me and became irate. This gentleman looked like your stereotypical gang banger with tattoos covering his arms, neck, and face.

Now driving side by side, he gave me the traditional one-finger salute, prompting me to return the gesture. While he was ascending the ramp, we continued to scream obscenities at each other as he started rolling down his window until spotting a police cruiser at the top of the ramp. As I drove off, it appeared the only reason he would have to roll down his window at that point was to take a shot at me without having to shoot through the glass. There but for the grace of God, go I.

I was in a recovery meeting one evening where a middle-aged woman was sharing her heart out. It was the sixth anniversary that her teenage son died from an overdose of heroin, the same drug she was using at the time. The amount of guilt, shame, and remorse this woman expressed was riveting and had all of us, except for two self-absorbed idiots sitting up front, with tears in our eyes.

They were only a few feet away from this woman, giggling and poking each other while sharing pictures and posts on their smartphones. I would argue those phones, as well as their owners, were not very smart at all. After watching this scenario unfold for a few minutes, I could not stand it any longer. The "Click," after being frozen in time for over a decade, came back to life.

I got out of my seat to have a chat with my two newly acquired resentments. Approaching my targets, I remembered one of our guiding principles: "Our common welfare should come first." I could not think of anything I was about to say or do that would add to our common welfare, so I bolted out of the meeting and went back home. This time, my "justified indignation" left me with a resentment I could not shake for several months.

Most of the time, my impulsive behavior only leads to different levels of embarrassment. I have been a member of a well-known massage chain for many years, privileged again to do something most people will never get to experience. The deal for membership is that "corporate" charges a monthly fee, taken automatically out of my credit card, entitling me to another sixty-minute massage.

Due to a hectic schedule, I could not make it in for several months and accumulated three one-hour sessions. My credit card number on file expired, and I neglected to call with my updated information. At my next appointment, the receptionist informed me I could not use any of the time I had accumulated as I was no longer considered an active member.

She asked for my new card number, which I did not have with me. I would need then to wait an hour or so until her supervisor, who was the only one who had the authority to override corporate, would arrive. Although I did not click, I did ask her to tell corporate to shove my membership where the sun does not shine.

Although I knew I would lose those 180 minutes, I walked out anyway. I later found out I could have paid for the massage in cash and kept all my credits if only I had the patience to wait and hear all my options.

I want to share one of the many ways I learned to deal with my anger issues. For my birthday one year, my wife purchased tickets for us to see the Dalai Lama speak in Long Beach, California, about a two-hour drive from San Diego. Her gift remains one of the most thoughtful I have ever received. On our way to Long Beach, however, we started bickering about things that did not matter. By the time we arrived at the venue, I was so angry I could not think straight.

One of the first things I heard the Dali Lama say was, "If you get angry at someone, become like a piece of wood." I believe His Holiness was suggesting we should not do or say anything to anyone until we can deal with the situation without anger. When we walked out of the venue that evening, I found a piece of driftwood I hung on to and stayed peaceful the entire ride home. I later made a necklace out of the wood I still wear today. It is a reminder that I get to choose how I will think, feel, or react in any given situation.

# 18

# THE IMAGINATION STATION

B Y NOW, I HOPE WE HAVE COME TO SOME understanding that it is our inner thoughts that shape our outer world. We must remember our thoughts are formative and live in that reality. We create everything twice—first in our minds and then in manifestation. The information we gather throughout the day gets processed by the ego, which will develop a game plan for us if we do not make one for ourselves.

Despite having this knowledge, most of us live our lives taking little or no responsibility for what we think. We go through life reacting to situations we believe need to conform to our way of thinking. Our perception of life is but a mirror image of our inner state of mind.

In Mathew 10:36 (KJV), Jesus said, "A man's foes are they of his own household," I do not believe Jesus was referring to our mothers, fathers, brother, and sisters. Our enemies, He said—are within our consciousness. So, when negative thoughts start filling the airwaves, we'd better tune in to a different frequency.

When we go through our days carrying negative feelings and aggressive thoughts, we will be met head-on by an equally hostile world. When we participate in life from a loving can-do consciousness, we will experience better opportunities and a greater sense of well-being.

Frank Wanderer, Ph.D., professor of psychology and author of numerous books on the power of the mind, writes, "The most important thing we need to know about the mind is that it is not something that exists separately, individually, like some inanimate object. The mind is not an object; it is a never-ending process of sorting through our dynamic stream of thoughts. Our minds are always evaluating and reevaluating things, categorizing them as either good or evil."

Dr. Wanderer adds, "Our mind is one of the most sophisticated and complicated instruments in the world. However, in this modern society, the mind is so bombarded with useless information, we have less time to consider the things we value. More of us are beginning to realize; we are more than our minds, thoughts, and emotions. When our attention no longer revolves around identifying with our personal history, we become more open to the deeper dimensions of our lives."

Before we can experience a new way of being, we must first develop a new way of thinking. Circumstances do not create thoughts. Our thoughts are the ego's perception of our experiences, and those perceptions can be off by miles. I believe the only way to overcome negative thoughts is by developing opposing ones more conducive to a healthy lifestyle.

In *the Power of Now*, Eckart Tolle writes, "What is the greatest obstacle to experiencing being? Identification with your own mind, which causes the thought to become compulsive. Not to be able to stop thinking is a dreadful affliction, but we do not realize this because almost everyone is suffering from it, so it is considered normal. This incessant mental noise prevents us from finding that realm of inner stillness that is inseparable from being."

Tolle adds, "Identification with our mind creates an opaque screen of concepts, labels, images, words, judgments, and definitions that block all true relationships. It comes between you and yourself, between you and your fellow man and woman, between you and nature, between you and God. It is this screen of thought that creates the illusion of separateness, the illusion that there is you and a totally separate other."

Our awakening is a continual process of clearing away the ego's counterproductive thoughts of fear, guilt, resentments, and self-pity that separate us from the ever-present now. All the books in the world cannot help us if we do not practice what we have learned. We must remain vigilant and let these simple spiritual principles guide our lives.

The truth is if we do not take responsibility for what we think, we will never be able to exercise our God-given freedom of choice. Thoughts by themselves remain just thoughts until the ego sifts through the information we provide and creates an impression of what it thinks is right. If our perceptions are corrupt, our lives will be as well. Our battles always begin within.

You may see a story like this on the show *Ripley's Believe It or Not*. A trainyard worker went into one of the freezer cars to clean it. When finished, he discovered he locked himself inside. The next day when his coworkers opened the door, they found the man's lifeless body inside. Looking for clues as to why this man died, they discovered his writing on the wall; "Cold, getting colder, freezing." This tragic death was even more poignant because the freezer unit on the car was not working. The man was frozen not by a machine but by his thoughts. Believe it or not.

An old Native American parable tells a story of two dogs who, at separate times, walk in and out of the same room. One of the dogs comes out wagging his tail, while the other leaves the room growling. A woman went in to see what could make one dog so happy and trigger such anger in the other. To her surprise, she finds a room full of mirrors. The happy dog found a thousand happy dogs looking back, while the other saw a thousand angry dogs growling. What we see in the mirror is just a reflection of who we are.

In *The Art of Original Thinking*, Jan Phillips, a Unity friend and author of many outstanding books, wrote, "Original thinking does not favor the letter of the law over the spirit of the law, or vice versa, but shapes a new and creative thought from the basic elements of the two. This is the alchemy of the creative process. It does not set hydrogen against oxygen but incorporates the two and yields water."

It is not what we see but how our egos interpret what we see that matters. Can you think of a time when your perception of a situation was in direct opposition to how others experienced it? We can have a hundred people looking at the same abstract piece of art and have one hundred different opinions on what the artist was trying to express.

On May 3, 2018, Kilauea, one of the world's most active volcanoes, located on the Big Island of Hawaii, erupted once again. Watching the news coverage of the fast-moving lava lake, I could not help but marvel at mother nature's beauty. Later in the newscast, a reporter interviewed a resident of the area, who hours before witnessed his home consumed by fire. I am sure his perception of the event was entirely different than the one I had.

We all see the world through individual filters, most of which we develop in childhood but continue to refine as we gather new information. Mark Twain quipped, "You can't depend on your eyes when your imagination is out of focus." When we focus on our misfortunes, we attract more of the same. When we focus on possibilities, opportunities will follow.

Most of us begin our lives holding on to the belief we are empty creatures sent out into the world to search for fulfillment. If this is our core belief, our lives then become the subtotal of what we have accumulated. To experience that elusive feeling of contentment, one must believe we are, first and foremost, living souls with unlimited potential to be discovered and released.

Believing in this process allows us to choose which master we serve today. We can choose courage over fear, love over hate, forgiveness over resentments, and gratitude over self-pity. This potential is always present, never absent, because there is no place where God is not.

I love the story about a group of monks who, in 1957, were relocating an ancient monastery in Thailand. While moving a giant clay statue of Buddha, one of the monks noticed a gaping hole in the figure's back. On closer examination, he saw a golden light emanating out of the darkness.

With hammer and chisel, the monk chipped away at the figure's exterior until revealing a statue of Buddha made of solid gold. Historians believe the Buddha was covered in mud by the monks several hundred years ago to protect it from the Burmese army. I know it sounds corny, but this is our story as well. We are all "golden Buddhas," covered in mud, waiting for the right time and place to let our light shine.

On a beautiful spring day, I walked along the beach with a friend who was berating herself about how she never got anywhere in life. I paused and asked her to look out on the horizon and visualize that she could sail to any destination in the entire world from that very spot. This simple shift of consciousness filled her with new hope and enthusiasm, at least for that day. Tomorrow will bring a whole new set of challenges for us to overcome.

In Proverbs 29:18 (KJV), we read, "Where there is no vision, the people perish." We cannot begin the next chapter of our lives if we keep reliving the previous ones. We must not allow ourselves to walk in ruts and routines. Dare to dream. Hold the image of what you truly desire and move in that direction. If we stop repeating our story as a sad one, it will eventually stop being one.

For our dreams to manifest the way we would like them, we must tell our story the way we would like it to be. The secret of manifestation lies solely in our imaginations. The dreams, hopes, and aspirations we hold for ourselves and others are what make our lives worth living.

Actor and comedian Jim Carrey shared a touching story about his late father. "My father could have been a great comedian, but he didn't believe it was possible for him. Instead, he got a safe job as an accountant.

"When I was twelve years old, he was let go from that same job, and our family had to do whatever we could to survive. I learned many great lessons from my father, not the least of which was you can fail at what you don't want, so you might as well take a chance on doing something you love."

Sometimes the bravest among us are the ones fighting battles the rest of us cannot see. When French actress Sarah Bernhardt had one of her legs amputated, she did not wallow in self-pity, thinking her career was over. She immediately began working on a new play where she assumed the part of a one-legged soldier. All of us possess the same ability to rise above our perceived limitations.

The most loving, kind, and understanding people I have ever encountered were busted up, bloodied, and bruised but found their way out of the muck and the mire. These folks understand and appreciate life, mainly due to their hardships that now fill them with love, compassion, and empathy for others.

When encountering obstacles, we sometimes lose sight of this fundamental force, but the light within us is always present because there is no place where God is not. However, the addicted mind (our egos) is a dream killer that practices not the Presence but the absence of God.

Jennifer Bricker was born in Romania and given up for adoption by her parents. An American couple from Illinois with three boys of their own adopted the little girl. Jennifer got raised believing she could do anything her brothers could do, and "can't" was not part of the family's vocabulary. From a young age, she dreamed of being a world-class gymnast and was glued to the television while watching women's gymnastics during the summer Olympics. Bricker had just one small challenge to overcome to fulfill her dream: she was born without legs.

Back in Illinois, climbing trees was one of Jennifer's favorite pastimes. She played sports, including baseball, basketball, and gymnastics. She started tumbling by learning how to perform acrobatic moves on a trampoline in her parents' backyard. She soon became Illinois state champion in tumbling.

Jennifer was interested in knowing more about her biological family. As it turned out, Olympic gymnast Dominique Moceanu was her biological sister. December 10, 2007, Jennifer said, was a day that "changed my world." She wrote to Dominique, including photographs and documents that left no doubt the two girls were siblings.

Jennifer reunited with both Dominique and another sister. While Jennifer remains close to her adoptive family, she has forged new bonds with her biological family. Bricker now performs as a professional aerialist and serves as a motivational speaker, sharing her incredible story with others. Jennifer's hope is "to inspire and motivate others to believe that anything is truly possible."

My good friend Manny once climbed Mount Kilimanjaro and hiked the Appalachian Trail. But now Emanual, a worldly and talented orthopedic surgeon, could not raise his body from where it lay. While taking an early morning bike ride, brake failure sent him careening down his driveway into a creek on the other side of the road. His head hit a rock, snapping it backward, bruising his spinal cord.

Speaking from his wheelchair, Manny remembers, "It was obvious I was paralyzed." His talented hands lay lifeless by his sides. Regarding his positive attitude toward life, the good doctor said, "You make it work. Rehabilitation does not change the injury, but it allows you to do the most with what you have left."

After a grueling rehabilitation, Manny went back to work as a medical consultant reviewing disability applications. He drives himself to work in a specially equipped minivan. Imagine applying for permanent disability due to carpal tunnel syndrome, and the orthopedic surgeon who will be reviewing your case is sitting in a wheelchair, still working, still active in his community, and still grateful to be alive.

Manny's wife made her transition a few years after the accident from a locally invasive brain tumor. In her final email to me, she wrote, "So as the old year closes, and on reflection, I believe that what makes life beautiful and worthwhile is people. It is the loving, generous family members and friends who have given us their positive thoughts, uplifting prayers, time, energy, and spirit, that keeps us moving forward."

Emanuel looks back on what he calls a "charmed life." He finds great value in his life-altering, near-death experience. "When you make yourself part of a community and try to make it better, it all comes back to you in your time of need."

In a recent note, he writes, "I have been fortunate once again to have fallen in love. I continue to volunteer at the medical school as a small group facilitator and do disability evaluations for Social Security." What a great example of the power we all have within us to overcome any of life's challenges.

Helen Keller stricken with a childhood illness described by her doctors as "acute congestion of the stomach and the brain" (most likely spinal meningitis), left her deaf, blind, and mute. Hellen, along with her teacher and lifelong companion, Anne Sullivan, made popular a communication system called braille, which continues to transform people's lives without sight worldwide.

Helen would later write, "The struggle of life is one of our greatest blessings. It makes us patient, sensitive, and godlike. It teaches us that although the world is full of suffering, it is also full of overcoming." Where we are, is the best possible place to get to where we want to be. Author C. JoyBell C. writes, "We can't be afraid of change. You may feel very secure in the pond that you are in, but if you never venture out of it, you will never know that there is such a thing as an ocean."

# 19

# INTEGRITY A CALL TO FREEDOM

IF YOU HAVEN'T YET NOTICED, WE LIVE IN A WORLD OF human relations. Our happiness or dissatisfaction in life will be determined by how well we relate to others. There is a purpose for everyone we encounter. They are here to teach us what we need to learn about ourselves. Some will bring happiness and joy, others stress and anxiety, but each will deliver what we need to know for the next stage in our development.

People who feel the need to control others' lives are usually incapable of managing their own. To feel included, insecure people tend to manufacture drama to get the attention they desire. The saddest people are those poor souls who live only to complain, judge, and criticize. It is vital to our emotional health that we do not allow these drama queens (male or female) to transfer their insecurities onto us.

Life is difficult, and we never know what trials and tribulations others may be facing. However, there is a vast difference between lending a sympathetic ear and getting sucked into a person's never-ending drama. If we genuinely wish to help someone stuck in the mud, we will need to plant our feet on solid ground and lift upward, not lay down with them.

Being open-minded is critical in the process of becoming a more conscientious human being. We must find common ground with others who may have different thoughts, customs, and beliefs than our own. Let us not worry about what others think, say, or do, or how they pray. Nothing will bring us greater peace of mind than minding our own damn business.

"Crabs in a Basket" is a way of thinking best described by Wikipedia: "If I can't have it, neither can you." While crabs placed in a basket could easily escape, their efforts would be in vain. When one crab starts its journey upward, the others grab hold of its hind legs to halt its progression. Thus, "mutually assured destruction" is once again guaranteed.

Betty Boop once said, "My mother always told me if you can't say anything nice, don't say anything at all. And some people wonder why I am so quiet around them!"

We must remember, no matter how deep we are in it, there is always a way out. We must stand up against those whose intent it is to keep us down. We should speak up and assert ourselves whenever necessary. This lesson was drilled into me by my mother, who I never saw back down from a fight.

My mother lived in one of the few apartment complexes in southwest Virginia, where dogs over sixty pounds were welcome. As I can attest from first-hand experience, when dogs this size defecate, they leave behind pounds of the stinky stuff. My mom was incensed that one of the neighborhood dogs dug up the flowerbeds she cared for so diligently.

When my mom was in her early eighties, she sent this email to the rest of the family. "Yesterday, I went outside to clean my windows and stepped into what I first believed was a bunch of wet leaves before it began oozing into my sneakers. It was quite a feat hopping into the bathroom on one leg after undergoing quadruple bypass surgery. Shit was everywhere. I called management, who said they were already working on this problem and doing their best.

"You know that answer did not sit right with me. That night I got out my flashlight and police whistle and waited. Sure enough, at 10 p.m., a German shepherd came prancing across the street and began digging in my flowerbed while its owner stood at the entrance of his building, smoking who knows what. I went outside, blew my whistle as hard as I could, and kept my flashlight on him until he and his dirty dog raced up the stairs taking shelter in their apartment.

"The following day, I called the office back and told them I could identify the dog and its owner and gladly testify in court. My terms for settlement are for the owner to apologize in writing and clean up after his mongrel. He must have thought I was a weak and sickly old lady and would allow his dog to violate my garden at will. No way, baby!"

Two English businessmen were preparing for the grand opening of their new clothing store the following day in London. The construction of the shop was finished months ago. There were shelves on the walls and racks on the floor, but not a stitch of clothing in sight. One of the owners said, "I'll bet any minute some thickheaded, dimwitted tourist is going to walk by and ask what we are selling."

Within moments, an elderly statesman walked up to the window, had a peek inside, and in a thick Irish brogue asked, "Well, lads, what are you selling here?" One of the owners walked up to him, and with no love lost, said, "We are selling arseholes." Without skipping a beat, the Irishman tipped his hat and replied, "So far, it looks like you guys are doing well—only two left."

Author and teacher Ernest Holmes said, "No individual can be happy who lives are in a continuous state of condemnation of people, conditions and things."

There is a silent addiction we all suffer from to some degree, the useless preoccupation we have with others. Judging others is the next great escape for those of us who are no longer chemically dependent but still need a way to escape their reality. Before we pass judgment on others, we had better first make sure our hands are clean. In one of the more practical teachings found in Mathew 5:7, Jesus suggests that before we try to remove the splinter from our brother's eye, we should first remove the plank from our own.

Carl Jung said, "If people can be educated to see the lowly side of their natures, they will learn to understand and love their fellow man. Less hypocrisy and a bit more tolerance can only have good results, for we are all too prone to transfer the injustice and violence we inflict upon ourselves to our neighbors."

Like me, do you pass judgment on others when stopped at a light, and the driver in front of you is on their phone, unaware the light has turned back to green? They look up just in time to get through the intersection themselves, leaving the rest of the pack behind.

On a picture-perfect day in San Diego, "Private Idaho," *one of my favorite* songs performed by the B-52s, came on the car radio. I pumped up the volume up to a ridiculously high level, oblivious of an ambulance stuck behind me with its lights flashing and sirens wailing. So really, who am I to judge?

One day a man in a parked car tossed a container with the remnants of his lunch out the passenger-side window. As I passed by, I picked up the discarded items and threw them back into the car. That is what makes this story funny. What makes it sad was that I was having a torrid affair with a married woman during that time. How is that for some good old-fashioned egocentric rationalization?

Whether in our personal lives or work environment, successful relationships start with the foundation of honesty, trust, and mutual respect. These are the building blocks required to develop healthy, long-lasting, mutually beneficial relationships. Others must feel confident that we will do what we say we will do and do it consistently.

Michelle Obama said, "We learned about honesty and integrity, that the truth matters, that you don't take shortcuts or play by your own set of rules. And success doesn't count unless you earn it fair and square." Integrity is doing the right thing for the right reason. We should be mindful that trust is a precious gift that takes years to build but destroyed in seconds by one stupid egocentric decision.

I have known men and women who, by example, demonstrate the ability to rise above the cattiness and selfishness predominant in our society today. Early in my recovery, my sponsor purchased a used Cadillac for $5,000, a lot of money back then. This car was in the repair shop more than it was on the road. The service costs were taking their toll on his bank account as well as his serenity. He gave the car away and took the loss instead of selling it to another unsuspecting individual.

Some of us (not me, of course) suggested we drive the Cadillac to the west side of Manhattan and leave it near one of the many chop shops in the area known to make cars disappear quicker than David Copperfield does during one of his live performances. Later, when I asked why he refused to let the insurance company take the hit, he said, "Recovery at what price, Sean?"

This lesson served me well a few years later when my uncle sold us his three-year-old Honda Civic for $3,700, which we could pay off in monthly installments. However, my uncle forgot to mention the vehicle had been stolen, taken for a joyride, and slammed into a commercial trash bin. It had extensive undercarriage damage, including a crack in the axle, which the repair shop "fixed" by welding it back together.

I am confident my uncle would never let us drive a car he knew to be dangerous but found it difficult to understand him not taking financial responsibility for the loss. My uncle made a killing in the stock market at an early age, buying into a little startup company called McDonald's. He was able to retire and live a comfortable life by the sea at the age of fifty-two.

Although I wanted to confront him, my goodhearted wife felt we should pay my uncle the full amount we agreed upon and move on. To do so, she offered the $1,200 she saved from doing manicures, pedicures, and body waxing in a salon in Soho to visit her family in Brazil. We gave him the remainder of the money in one lump sum and moved on.

We found out later just how much my uncle appreciated this gesture. After dinner one evening, he pulled me aside to talk in private. He told me he admired how we handled the situation with the car, and despite the circumstances, we never showed animosity toward him. He wanted us to know that we did not have to worry about our kids' college fund, for he put enough money aside to pay for it in full.

About twenty years ago, I evaluated a patient to offer an opinion if I believed surgery was a reasonable option for him. This young man, who just turned twenty, suffered from years of debilitating low back pain due to a significant deformity (grade 3 spondylolisthesis) in his lumbar spine. He tried all the recommended conservative modalities with little or no improvement.

The patient knew he had run out of options and needed the procedure but was terrified about surgery. He would require an L4–5 anterior/posterior spinal fusion, a routine operation to perform, but a long and arduous rehabilitation for the patient. This gentleman and his girlfriend, who came to every appointment with him, had matted-down blue, green, and yellow hair with more piercings than I have ever seen up to that point.

I smiled and said to him, "Dude, growing up, it would have been more dangerous for me walking the streets of my neighborhood looking like you than to undergo this procedure."

We all had a good laugh, and I could tell he was starting to relax. Now he was the one smiling. He wanted to make a deal. He would go ahead with the proposed surgery if I let him and his girlfriend dye my hair blue on one of his postoperative visits. Believing he would never remember such a thing, I gave him my word.

I am happy to report this young man did exceptionally well. I was not sure if he remembered my promise, but his girlfriend sure did. On his first postoperative visit, they advised me to get ready;

they would keep me to my word. I believed I could outsmart them by booking my haircut appointments to coincide with his clinic visits every six weeks. However, they stopped by unannounced one morning for the sole purpose of coloring my hair.

That afternoon I had a lunchtime meeting with a local orthopedic surgeon interested in referring all his spinal patients to our practice. It was a big deal, and I had to be on point. The patient and his girlfriend looked heartbroken as I was giving them my buts and whys, knowing all along it was not the right thing to do.

I slipped into panic mode when the patient looked up and said, "But you gave me your word."

My thought was to let them color my hair asap, so I would have time to run home and shower it out before the meeting. I did just that and shampooed my hair a half dozen times until the water going down the drain was clear. When I looked in the mirror, I felt sick to my stomach. My darker navy-blue hair turned into a striking pastel blue. I later found out they purposely bleached my hair before adding the color. This way, it would not wash out.

I knew jumping back into the shower would be an exercise in futility, so I got dressed and made my way to the restaurant where the meeting was taking place. Unbeknownst to me, some of our staff members who arrived earlier explained to the good doctor why I was running a little late.

As I came through the door, the doctor stood up and shook my hand. He told me how much he enjoyed the story behind the coloring of my hair. He later informed our business manager he would be delighted to refer his patients to a practice that operates in this manner.

When I think of people who lived their lives with integrity, I think of men like Mohammad Ali, Nelson Mandela, Martin Luther King Jr., and Mahatma Gandhi. These were men who put aside personal ambition to work for the common good of all people. Men who stuck to their vision come hell or high water speaking out against the injustice they saw in the world.

Mahatma Gandhi is best known as the leader of the Indian independence movement against British rule. Employing nonviolent civil disobedience techniques, Gandhi led India to independence and inspired other civil rights movements worldwide.

After graduating from law school in April 1893, Gandhi set sail for South Africa. Because of his heritage, he faced the same blatant discrimination that all non-white citizens endured. He spent twenty-six years in South Africa, developing his deep spiritual convictions about the equality of all men. Gandhi hoped for an independent India based on religious pluralism, a policy respecting the diversity of religious beliefs coexisting within its society.

Gandhi's vision was challenged by a new Muslim nationalism, demanding a separate Muslim homeland carved out of India. In August 1947, Britain granted independence but partitioned the land into a Hindu-majority India and Muslim-majority Pakistan, which remains in place today.

Gandhi was eventually arrested and convicted of treason. While in prison, the British government enacted a new law granting the "untouchable caste" a separate electorate. In protest, Gandhi began a fast-unto-death. He urged his people to stop cooperating with the government. He advised they neither kill nor injure British citizens but be willing to suffer and die for the cause.

Intense public scrutiny forced the British government to compromise and released him from prison. On January 30, 1948, Gandhi was on his way to address a prayer meeting when a Hindu nationalist fired three rounds from a 9mm pistol into his chest at point-blank range. He died from his wounds a short time later.

While reporting on Gandhi's funeral, Edward R. Murrow, an American broadcast journalist, spoke these words: "The object of this massive tribute died as he has always lived: a private man without wealth, without property, without an official title or office. Mahatma Gandhi was not the commander of armies nor a ruler of vast lands. He could not boast of any scientific achievements or artistic gift, yet men, governments, and dignitaries from all around the world have joined hands today to pay homage to this little brown man in the loincloth who led his country to freedom."

Born July 18, 1918, Nelson Rolihlahla Mandela was a South African antiapartheid activist recognized internationally as an icon of social justice. A young Nelson remembers the stories of his ancestors' courage and sacrifice in the resistance against the Apartheid regime. Nelson felt called to join the struggle. This systemic government-sponsored segregation divided South Africa along racial lines from 1948 until the early 1990s.

Mandela was arrested in 1962 and subsequently convicted of conspiring to overthrow the government and sentenced to life imprisonment. He was facing the death penalty when on April 20, 1964, he gave his famous "Speech from the Dock." The dock is the small, partitioned area held by a defendant in a court of law. These are the final words of Mandela's speech, which have become immortalized.

"I have fought against white domination, and I have fought against black domination. I have cherished the ideal of a democratic and free society in which all persons live together in harmony and with equal opportunities. It is an ideal which I hope to live for and to achieve. But if needs be, it is an ideal for which I am prepared to die."

Mandela never wavered in his devotion to a free and democratic South Africa. He served twenty-seven years in prison before growing domestic and international pressure forced President Frederik Willem de Klerk to release him in 1990.

As he walked out of prison, Mandela spoke these words of comfort to a concerned nation, "The time for the healing of wounds has come." Mandela became the country's first elected president in a fully representative democratic South Africa. Reminiscing, Mandela said, "I knew if I didn't leave my bitterness and hatred behind, I'd still be in prison. For to be free is not merely to cast off one's chains, but to live in a way that respects and enhances the freedom of others."

The Reverend Martin Luther King Jr. became the most visible spokesperson for the civil rights movement from 1954 until he was shot to death on a hotel balcony in Memphis on April 4, 1968. Inspired by Mahatma Gandhi's activism, Dr. King is known for his work in advancing the civil rights of African Americans through nonviolent civil disobedience.

King's most challenging time must have come on Sunday, September 15, 1963. On that day, four members of the KKK bombed the Sixteenth Street Baptist Church in Birmingham, Alabama, killing four young African American girls and wounding many others. King returned three days after the bombing to eulogize the four girls. To the dismay of many in the African American Community, King's message continued to be one of nonviolence.

Born in segregated Louisville, Kentucky, on January 17, 1942, Mohammad Ali was the first fighter in boxing history to win the world heavyweight championship on three separate occasions. In 1964, at age twenty-two, he won the title by knocking out Sonny Liston in one of the biggest upsets in boxing history. Soon after becoming the champ, he joined the Nation of Islam and changed his name from Cassius Clay, which he referred to as his "slave name," to Muhammad Ali.

When notified by the Selective Service he was eligible for the draft, Ali applied for a conscientious objector status based on his membership in the Nation of Islam. Ali's announcement came when most people in the States still supported the war in Southeast Asia. Many Americans vehemently condemned Ali's stand.

Commenting on the case, Ali said, "I strongly object to the fact that so many newspapers have given the American public and the world the impression that I have only two alternatives in taking this stand, either I go to jail or go to the army. There is another alternative, and that alternative is justice." He added, "In the end, I am confident that justice will come my way, for the truth must eventually prevail."

On June 20, 1967, by refusing to be inducted into the US Armed Forces, Ali got convicted of violating the US Selective Service laws.

The champ would say, "Man, I don't have a quarrel with them, Vietcong."

Mohamad was stripped of his heavyweight title, fined $10,000, and sentenced to five years in prison. Ali versus the United States appealed to the US Supreme Court, which overturned his conviction in a unanimous decision on June 28, 1971.

After a four-year hiatus, Ali returned to the ring and knocked out heavyweight champion George Foreman at the end of the eighth round during the "Rumble in the Jungle" to regain the heavyweight title. He lost his belt to a novice twenty-four-year-old Leon Spinks, a ten-to-one underdog. In a rematch seven months later, Ali regained the title in a unanimous fifteen-round decision at Madison Square Garden (MSG).

Around that time, I was working in an upscale hotel about a mile north of MSG. After the first fight, I recognized the otherwise unrecognized new heavyweight champion enter the lobby, and I asked for an autograph. A gentleman walking next to the champ replied, "Sorry, we don't sign anything," and walked away.

On the contrary, a few hours later, Mohamad Ali walked out of the elevator doors into the lobby and was quickly surrounded by a group of adoring African American children dressed in matching school uniforms. Ali was handing out what I believed to be $100 bills, having the kids jump high into the air and snatch them out of his hand. When he saw me standing in the background with pen and paper in hand, he maneuvered his way through the children and asked, "Would you like me to sign that for you?"

Although I did not get any cash that day, I still have that little scrap of paper with Mohammed Ali's name inscribed on it. I look at it every so often to remind myself of the great lesson I learned that day. Being a champion is not what a fighter accomplishes inside the ring, but how he lives his life and treats others outside the ring. In this regard, Mohammad Ali was "The Greatest" of all time.

# 20

# WALLS AND BRIDGES

AUTHOR AND TV PERSONALITY IYANLA VANZANT wrote, "Until you heal the wounds of your past, you will continue to bleed. You can bandage the bleeding with food, with alcohol, with drugs, with woodwork, with cigarettes, with sex, but eventually, it will ooze through the stain of your life. You must find the strength to open the wounds, stick your hands inside, pull out the core of the pain that is holding you in your past, the memories, and make peace with them."

If we do not do some housecleaning, it will be difficult for us to stay in the ever-present moment, which is the only place where the ego lies dormant. The past negative energy we accepted into our consciousness must find its way to a resolution if we wish to be free. We must look back and forgive when necessary and make amends whenever possible. We all have challenges, and we never know what others may be facing. We are all fighting separate battles in the same egocentric war.

One of the more self-defeating emotions we hold on to more tenaciously than any other is guilt. We may feel guilty for something we have done or left undone. Much of our guilty feelings result from what we see as our failure to live up to someone else's expectations. We can rid ourselves of guilt and resentment, both of which have their origins in the past, by unleashing the spiritual principles of forgiveness and restitution.

Sigmund Freud theorized, "Guilt proceeds the act you feel guilty of doing. It does not come from real or supposed transgression; the transgression comes from the sense of guilt. It is consciousness out pictured." Those addicted are more likely to linger in a cesspool of guilt, which offers no benefit whatsoever unless it helps us move in a new positive direction. Restitution relieves our troubled souls from the hauntings of egos past and helps us understand the importance of living honorable lives in the here and now.

In Matthew 18:21 (NIV), we read that Peter (Jesus's favorite disciple) was angry and unwilling to let it go. He asked Jesus, "Lord, how many times shall I forgive my brothers who sin against me? Up to seven times?"

Jesus responded by saying we should forgive "seventy times seven," a number He used to symbolize infinity. We must always forgive, no matter how grievous the offense. Forgiveness is not something we do to give aid to the perpetrator but in and for ourselves.

We can all get caught up in the moment and do or say things we later regret. My favorite Bible story is in Matthew 21:12-13 (NIV) when Jesus went into the temple and overthrew the moneychanger's tables. He said to them, "My house shall be called a house of prayer, but ye have made it into a den of thieves." No matter how you look at this, Jesus lost His cool.

In trying to explain Jesus's reaction to this event, biblical scholars have referred to His outburst in the temple as "righteous indignation." I love this story because if Jesus could lose His composure in the high state of consciousness he was in, then there is hope for a society of men and women, just like you and me, in which Jesus was once a proud member.

When we let our guard down, we can easily fall prey to the ego's never-ending projections of fear and judgments. We may find ourselves on the same level of consciousness Jesus found Himself in upon entering the temple. Whether you are on the giving or receiving end of a scenario like this, both parties will have centering work to do.

Once upon a time, two brothers who were owners of adjoining cattle ranches in the heartland had their first dispute in over forty years. For decades they worked side-by-side, sharing machinery, goods, and labor. Their longtime collaboration fell apart one day by what appeared to be a minor misunderstanding that got way out of hand.

On the morning before the older brother left on a three-day fishing trip, there was a knock on the door. On the other side was a man carrying a toolbox looking for a few days' works. Still fuming over his younger brother's misdeeds, he brought the carpenter down to the creek that separated the two properties. He explained the situation with his brother and instructed the carpenter to build a six-foot-high wooden fence along the property line.

When the older brother returned from his trip, he was outraged by what he saw. Instead of a fence, the carpenter built a wooden bridge over the creek, complete with brass handrails. As the older brother came down the hill to give the carpenter a piece of his mind, the younger brother came running up from the opposite direction with outstretched arms.

They met in the center of the bridge. The younger brother was the first to speak. "It must have been difficult for you to build this bridge, after what I've said and done." They stood there, hugging and telling stories of the week past as the carpenter was packing up his gear, getting ready for his next destination.

The brothers asked if he could stay to work on some additional projects. As the carpenter threw his toolbox over his shoulder, he said, "I would like to stay, but there are others out there that can use a carpenter's hand to build bridges instead of walls."

I love the message behind the Broadway musical *Joseph and the Amazing Technicolor Dreamcoat*, an adaptation of a story found in Genesis. It is a tale about Joseph and his sinister brothers who sold Joseph into slavery. But Joseph, who had the power to interpret dreams, fell in favor with Pharaoh. He made his way up the ladder to become the Prime Minister of Egypt, answering only to Pharaoh himself.

Around that time, a great famine struck the surrounding cities of Egypt. Caravans traveled great distances to buy grain from Joseph, who was now in charge of everything. When his brothers were facing starvation, they also came to Egypt looking for assistance. Joseph was most forgiving about his enslavement and said to them, "You may have intended it for evil, but God intended it for good."

Today, the need for me to make amends are few and far between. My judgments, however, continue uninterrupted. Healing takes place by those of us sick and tired of listing to the nonsense we tell ourselves. However, it is now time for a classic Irish tale about my father and the incredible transformative power of forgiveness.

When my father was in his early seventies, he received a diagnosis of stage four pancreatic cancer. He lingered in the hospital for a month before taking his last breath. A year before this admission, he fractured his femur and was put in traction and hospitalized for several months. His doctors refused to administer alcohol and detoxed him using the pain medication and muscle relaxers he required for his broken leg.

To his credit, my father did not consume any alcohol throughout his final year here on earth and did it, he said, "Without that AA crap." So, what happens to an addict who gets clean but does not participate in a recovery program?

A few days before his passing, my father called me over to his bedside. I believed I was finally going to hear those elusive words—"I love you"—come out of his mouth. Verbatim, these are the last words my father ever spoke to me. He said, "My son, I'm seventy-two years old, and I could still get it up." I guess "good news" comes in a variety of ways!

The first official amends I made was to a relative who let me borrow his car for a night out with the boys in the height of my addiction. I told the story that I was heading back to the beach area when a pickup truck hauling a twenty-foot sailboat came out of nowhere. I said there was sand on the road, and when I hit the brakes, the car went airborne, ending its flight by wrapping itself around a tree. Not a bad story, if I do say so myself, but just not the truth.

The truth is, I was stoned out of my mind and fell asleep at the wheel. I explained what happened that night and asked how much I owed him for the car. He said, "I am very proud of what you have done to change your life around, and the only amends I would ask of you is to remain my friend forever," for which thirty-five years later, I continue to do.

We must be discerning when going back to make our amends. We must check our motives, and best run it by someone who has experience in this process. I placed women on my list where my intention was not to change my behavior but to hook back up with them again. There was no need for me to make amends to those who ran the streets with me. The dog-eat-dog mentality that ruled the hood was all part of the gig.

Our focus should center first on those relationships closest to us. Our family and friends take the brunt of our insanity during, and sometimes long after, active addiction. I believe we also need to put our names on the list to remember the grievous harm we caused ourselves. We must learn to forgive what we perceive as unforgivable. We must not sweep any financial amends we may owe under the carpet if we wish to continue moving forward.

I met John Lennon for the first time at the New York Hilton in 1971. I had always been a big fan of the Beatles and connected with John's music as a solo artist. As I walked past the Hilton's Grand Ballroom, I heard what sounded like Lennon's newest hit, "Imagine," playing. Peeking inside expecting to see a cleaning crew blasting a boom box, John was on stage with the rest of his band rehearsing for a show to be aired the following evening.

As I was still using drugs at that time, I did not think twice about pulling up a chair and watching the rehearsal. As the workers scurried about getting ready for the following day, I had a front-row seat to one of the greatest shows on earth. When the band took a break, I walked up to John, who was more than welcoming and introduced myself. I stood there for a few awkward moments, and as I had no pen or paper in hand, John thanked me for stopping by and walked back to be with the rest of the band.

That evening I checked out two books from the local library, *Lennon Remembers* and *In His Own Write*, written by John, consisting of short stories, drawings, and poetry. For the millennials out there, a library was just like Starbucks is today but without the coffee and danish.

The following morning, I arrived at the hotel early with books in hand, hoping to get John, one of the greatest songwriters who ever lived, to autograph them for me. I could not believe my luck. Lennon's band was back on stage, this time for a dress rehearsal. While the group was taking a break, I walked up to John and re-introduced myself.

Once again, Lennon was more than gracious. As John was signing the first book, one of his bandmates shouted, "Hey, Johnny, what are you doing?"

Lennon replied, "A repetition of a repetition," which drew chuckles from everyone. He handed me the second book and asked if there was anything else. As I stood there starstruck and dumbfounded, Lennon turned around, walked backstage, and disappeared.

So, what does any of this have to do with practicing the principle of restitution? After I got clean in 1985, I realized the public library was still the books' rightful owner. Lennon not only autographed these books for me but drew in caricatures and dated them in

Japanese. I talked it over with the librarian, who said I could purchase both books at the used book discounted price of six dollars and forty cents. Boo-yah!

Making amends is not merely apologizing for what we have done but changing the behavior necessitating the amends. When it came to my immediate family, there were not many specific amends I needed to make. Except for some chump-change I snatched out of my father's pockets; I never stole much in material value from my family. It was my nonparticipation within the family structure I needed to change. I would attend most family gatherings but head straight into the bedroom and sleep until everyone left.

As a father of two adult children, I cannot imagine what it must have been like for my mother, who had four other children to raise, to deal with the likes of me. Although never sent to prison, I was in and out of jails, institutions, and consciousness throughout my active addiction. As well as the usual emergency room visits for broken bones, cuts, and bruises, my mom had to deal with some unique childrearing situations.

It seems I always found myself in the wrong place at the wrong time. When I was twelve, one of the younger boys in our building ran around our garden area with a plastic spray bottle. Whatever he sprayed began smoking. Curious, I hopped the fence, taking the container away from the boy, warning him to go home before his parents found out what he was doing.

I sprayed everything in sight: bushes, bottles, cans, and dirty diapers, everyday items found in our garden area. I was having a blast until I started to feel a burning sensation in the middle of my chest. As I ran my fingers over the affected area, my skin peeled off in layers like peeling an onion. My right hand, which held the container, was burning so severely I screamed out loud for help.

I ran to the neighborhood pharmacist, who back then treated minor injuries. But as the container showed this was hydrochloric acid we were dealing with, the pharmacist called an ambulance that took me to the local hospital. My mom, who once again left work early to come to my rescue, arrived quickly.

The doctors there said they were ill-equipped to handle this type of emergency and arranged for my transfer to a level one trauma center on the east side of Manhattan. My mother would later say one of the doctors told her if treatment failed, there was a possibility I could lose my hand.

One evening I was hanging out pitching quarters with a group of friends when a car turned the corner, and someone sitting in the backseat fired half a dozen shots into the crowd. I got hit once in the right elbow, and one hit me directly in the center of my back. These were only pellets fired from an air-powered co2 rifle, causing more fear and anger than any real harm.

The pellets stung for only a few minutes, and there was hardly any bleeding. However, the paramedics insisted I go to the hospital since both projectiles made contact with bone. I was only seventeen at the time, so my mom would once again have to meet me in the emergency room before receiving any treatment. I asked my friend Frankie to tell my mother I twisted my ankle and needed to go to the hospital to get some x-rays.

Frankie, the least athletic among us, ran up the five flights of stairs to our apartment and pounded on the door. When my mother answered, he was holding onto the wall hyperventilating but was finally able to spit out, "Sean got shot, and they need you at the hospital right away."

As a parent, I can only imagine the terror my mother felt at that moment. When she arrived at my bedside, she looked as if she was going to collapse. It took less than a day for me to recover from my injuries, but I have a feeling Mom was not so lucky.

A few years ago, my current wife of twenty-eight years, without giving any context whatsoever, informed me she searched the internet to see whatever came of my first wife, Sabrina. Although I did not object to her curiosity, I did not see the point in doing so. If I were to contact Sabrina now, after forty years of silence, I would likely scare the living hell out of her, doing more harm than good, a no-no in recovery.

I first met "Sabi," a gentle soul with Sicilian roots, during the summer of seventy-four. She wrote a daily entry in a notebook outlining our time together and presented it to me on our first anniversary. I still have that notebook and do not have to read far into it to see the grievous harm I caused this poor woman, whose only crime was falling in love with the likes of me.

In one of her entries, Sabrina wrote, "I hope you're all right. Last night I could hardly sleep. I was, and still am, worried about you. On the phone, you sounded like you were going to commit another one of those crimes. I know you are a professional, but I don't want to see you get hurt." Her words were prophetic, as that was the day I got pistol-whipped for being twenty minutes late for a meeting.

Soon after we married, I invited two of my associates over for dinner. Sabrina was a great cook, and that night she outdid herself by making a juicy roast with potatoes and vegetables in the oven. However, that night one of our guests broke my golden rule of association—no weapons allowed in the house.

Out of the corner of my eye, I caught a glimpse of a small 22-caliber revolver placed on the counter separating the living room from the kitchen, which I quickly made disappear. I am not sure if my wife saw the pistol or not, but her demeanor changed radically after that.

She placed the roast on the table and asked me to come into the kitchen to help. As the "head of the family," I was responsible for carving the meat when it came out of the oven. As Sabrina was fixing the vegetables, I reached into a drawer behind her and pulled out a large carving knife to cut the roast.

As I did so, the blade scraped other utensils in the drawer, making a loud screeching noise that caused her to jump. As there were only us two in the kitchen, I got the impression that Sabrina thought I was going to stab her in the back. She filed for divorce soon after, probably one of the best decisions she ever made.

In December 2016, while sending out Christmas cards, I came across the fruit of my wife's earlier investigation. In front of me was a note complete with Sabrina's new married name and current address. Damn the internet. Now I had to decide what to do, considering I might increase the damage I caused if I contacted her, and I was unwilling to do so.

Sabrina was the only person left on my original list of people I needed to make amends to but never reached out for the reasons stated above. I sent her a somewhat ambiguous season greetings card wishing her and her family well. I added the chapter I wrote about our old neighborhood where we used to walk the streets holding hands.

I received a card back from her that year. She wrote, "God is good. It sounds like you've had a miraculous healing." She said she enjoyed my writings and hoped to read more of the book someday. I sent her another card in 2017 without a response. The one I sent for Christmas 2018 came back with a return to sender sticker on the envelope. I do not know what happened on her end, but my healing was in the effort, as it is with everything in recovery.

# 21

# LOVE LUST OR BUST

IF YOU COME FROM A DYSFUNCTIONAL FAMILY SUCH AS mine, where addictive behavior was considered normal, developing healthy relationships will not come easy. Children will often mimic the dysfunction they see within their family and carry that behavior into adulthood. If their maladaptive personality traits remain untreated, they will more than likely pass them on to the next generation and so on. Those abused as children will often become the abusers and remain so until they surrender to their dysfunction and co-create a new norm.

When I first placed relationships as a topic I wanted to discuss in this book, I nixed the idea several times. My history in this area has been less than admirable and more than embarrassing. As healthy relationships hold the key to experiencing a happy life, I will put my fear of judgment aside and share some of my personal experiences for whatever they are worth.

I want to begin by revealing some relationship choices I made before cleaning up my act. This way, I can concentrate on the more significant relationships we have with our families, friends, and, most importantly, the relationship we have with our higher self. Unfortunately, I grew up believing the more intimate the relationship, the deeper the hurt, and to be honest, this was one area where I already hit maximum capacity.

By the time I entered puberty, I was petrified of women. I was interested in all the little bumps and curves the girls our age was developing but felt that misery was sure to follow if I connected with them on an emotional level. Physically, although a little lean, I was not a bad looking guy and had no problem attracting ladies but would always do something to sabotage the relationship.

I developed a philosophy that all women were liars and cheats, not to be trusted. So, like everything concocted by the ego, I went out to prove its validity. I shied away from emotionally stable girls and gravitated towards those from other dysfunctional families who, when I looked in their eyes, there was nobody home.

Although I made it to first and second base several times, I was a junior in high school the first time I ever hit a home run. A senior at the school called to tell me she was babysitting that evening and invited me over to have some fun.

The bases have changed somewhat over the years. Now, oral sex, which was considered third base in my time, has been pushed back to first base, where it is now considered "just kissing." I do not know if I want to know what the millennials would nowadays call hitting a homer.

I took the young lady up on her offer. Once inside, she said we did not have much time and better get down to business. I do not remember if we even kissed that night, but I remember how awkward I felt taking off my clothes in front of her. She took my hand and laid on the sofa, pulling me on top of her. Within seconds I found myself sliding into home base, and in less than a minute, the game was over.

Although a little embarrassed by my performance that evening, I felt somewhat relieved that God finally answered my prayers and let me hit a ball out of the park. But there is an old saying: "Be careful what you pray for; you just might get it." I got it all right. It came in the form of the astrological sign represented by the symbol of the crab. These little creatures invaded my private parts and seemed most content chewing on my ball sack.

*Pthirus pubis*, a.k.a. pubic lice, are small parasites that attach to the skin and hair around your genitals. They feed exclusively on blood. The most common sign of pubic lice is intense genital itching. I panicked when I saw these little creatures crawling about my manhood and once again ran to our local pharmacist for advice. He prescribed an over-the-counter Lindane lotion he said was safe and effective when used according to the label's instructions.

I ran home with my new pharmacist-recommended chemical weapon in hand to begin my battle to kill the beasts. The instructions were easy to follow. It included an asterisk at the bottom of the page that advised, if the infestation was severe, shave the area before application. Although I could only count a half dozen of these little crotch critters, that was severe enough for me.

I shaved my affected area, leaving a series of little nicks along the way. When I applied the lotion, it felt as though I placed a blow torch on my testicles. I hopped into the bathtub and ran cold water directly from the faucet over my genitals, unable to stop the flow even for a minute to call for an ambulance. The lesson I learned that day was that women not only have the power to crush you emotionally but can send plagues of biblical proportions your way.

After my first marriage ended, I met a twenty-two-year-old divorced mother of a five-year-old boy. She and I began dating during my self-imposed exile in the Rockaways. One day while eating watermelon, my new girlfriend insisted I not swallow the seeds as they could grow in my stomach. She also told me over dinner one evening that some women in her culture put a portion of their menstrual flow in a man's food to get him to marry her.

As I had no interest in remarrying, this was the last meal I ever shared with this young lady. I will not bore you with additional stories about my relationship during my active addiction. However, it is safe to assume that it was more of the same, one unavailable fruitcake after another.

My attraction to women was based solely on their sexual prowess and ability to perform. Long legs, nicely shaped breasts, and a bad-ass butt were more important than a beautiful smile, crystal clear eyes, and an upbeat personality. Unfortunately, my pattern of choosing unhealthy women followed me well into my recovery.

In the recovery movement, we often hear that if you are not in an existing relationship, do not get involved in one for the first year. Next to total abstinence from all drugs, I believe spending time getting to know ourselves should be our next priority. Besides taking the focus away from where it is needed most, relationships bring up all sorts of insecurities that makes one more vulnerable to relapse.

At six months clean, I hooked up with a woman who was also in early recovery, forgetting the golden rule of no relationships for the first year. I rationalized I was not looking to get involved in a "relationship," but this lady was super attractive, and I could not pass up an opportunity like this.

On the way up to my apartment, I realized this would be the first time I would be having sex without an abundance of chemicals in my system, and I panicked when it came time to do the deed. After this encounter that very well could have ended in relapse, I spent the next three years working on myself, and I am so glad I did.

When I felt ready, I placed an ad in *Rolling Stone* magazine's classified section, one of the few publications offering dating services through advertisements. I received more than a dozen responses, most from professional women, including an architect, a nurse, a paralegal, and a woman who owned a dance studio in midtown Manhattan.

The woman I chose to be the love of my life was doing time in a Florida state prison for pulling a pistol on a police officer. I had four years clean at the time. Could you imagine the choices I made when I was getting loaded? I knew I needed to reexamine this dating thing after sending my lady friend in prison $100 for the bus ride to New York to come and live with me.

My next date was with a twenty-eight-year-old lesbian who wanted to have a romantic relationship with a man for the first time. That little voice inside my head was screaming, *don't do it, Sean, don't do it,* but of course, I did it. To make a long story short, my friend in prison would remain there for many years to come. The lady I was dating on the outside went back to her lesbian lover within a couple of weeks.

I was more than frustrated with my current dating situation and came to believe God's will and my will were moving in opposite directions. Once again, I needed to surrender to God's will, which I now believed was to become a Unity minister. And surrender I did. Two weeks later, I met my current wife of twenty-eight years, raised two healthy nonaddicted children, and have lived out the American Dream.

To make room for healthy relationships, we must first acknowledge that some of the people we are attached to are unquestionably pathological. The biggest challenge we face is determining which ones are salvageable and which ones need to go. Remember, those "friends" of ours who gossip about others will also be talking behind our backs. My suggestion would be to get rid of them first.

It matters not if they are family members or childhood friends. We must not let guilt stop us from removing noxious people from our lives. We need to learn how to walk away from anyone that threatens our peace of mind. Not allowing superficial people to put the weight of their inadequacies on our backs is vital to our mental health. If a person cannot accept you for who you are and continues to misrepresent you, they need to go.

For many people, the only way they feel complete is by having a partner by their side. There is nothing wrong with having a partner, but it becomes an issue when we find that special someone but lose ourselves in the process. Being with no one is better than being with the wrong person. Remember, loneliness is a deficiency of the spirit.

We must once again reconnect with our higher self to rectify the deficiency.

I delight in the writings of Khalil Gibran. In *The Prophet*, Gibran writes, "Love one another but make not a bond of love. Let it rather be a moving sea between the shores of your souls. Fill each other's cup but drink not from one cup. Give one another of your bread but eat not from the same loaf. Sing and dance together and be joyous, but let each one of you be alone, even as the strings of a lute are alone though they quiver with the same music."

Gibran continues, "Give of your hearts but not into each other's keeping. For only the hand of Life can contain your hearts. And stand together, yet not too near together; for the pillars of the temple stand apart. And the oak tree and cypress tree grow not in each other's shadow. Let there be spaces in your togetherness and let the winds of the heavens dance between you."

Many who marry believing it would end their loneliness realize they feel just as lonely having a partner as they did without one. Overcoming feelings of loneliness remains an inside job. We must first develop a loving relationship with ourselves before connecting with others in a meaningful way. If we do not, we will not bridge the separation we feel, which is always rationalized by the ego.

One can feel lonely standing in the middle of a crowd, while others may find themselves alone but feel connected to the entire universe. There is a story about an Eastern mystic who lived in a cave high in the Himalayas Mountains, renowned for his spiritual awareness. A reporter went up the mountain to interview the man and asked, "Are you not lonely being up here all by yourself?" The mystic replied, "I didn't feel lonely until you came."

We should invite only those people who are kind and compassionate along with us on our journey. We should choose men and women of character that we admire and reflect the type of person we aspire to be. We should give little or no attention to what people say but judge them by how they treat the most unfortunate among us.

Start spending time with healthy-minded individuals, people who believe in you, and help lift your spirits when you feel down. The German philosopher Johann Wolfgang von Goethe said, "If we take people as they are, we make them worse. If we see them as they were meant to be, we help make them all that they can be."

We should strive to develop at least one meaningful relationship with an individual who we perceive to be at a higher state of consciousness than ourselves and share all our fears, hopes, and aspirations with them. Remember, it is Truth, not trivia, that will set us free.

When we awaken to our authentic selves, we will be progressively less interested in participating in the superficial. Johnny Depp, a.k.a. Jack Sparrow, Edward Scissorhands, and Willy Wonka, said, "There are four questions of value in life. What is sacred? Of what is the spirit made? What is worth living for, and what is worth dying for?"

The answer to all four of these questions, he said, is love. The million-dollar question is, however, what is love? How do we define it? Like God, love is not definable but is an observable phenomenon of the human experience. Our need is not to go out seeking love, for love is not lost; we are!

The poet Hafiz said, "Love sometimes gets tired of speaking sweetly, and wants to rip the shreds out of your erroneous notions that make you fight within yourself and with others, causing the world to weep on too many fine days." Although I cannot define love, I want to share what I believe are the three types of love we can experience.

In Greek mythology, Eros is the god of erotic love and desire. When hormones are surging during puberty, most of us have experienced love in this capacity, a self-centered love that desires not to give but to possess. Loving in this manner is nothing more than a symbiotic attachment. Love is not dependent on an object of desire but is a state of consciousness. What we commonly call falling in love is, in most cases, a falling out of love and another victory for the ego.

Philia love is a brotherly love we tend to give to those we consider deserving of it, depending on how well they serve our interests. Philia love was palpable throughout this country after September 11, 2001, when our airplanes were turned into missiles and brought our vulnerability as a country up-front and personal. Neighbors began talking with neighbors again, and courtesy was the rule, not the exception, on the highways.

Agape love is a transcendent force. It is the activity of God, which is everywhere present at every point in time. Again, is there anywhere God is not? Agape love seeks not its own but relishes in the joy of giving for its own sake. Agape love looks beyond appearances, seeing only the good in people. We can always tap into this divine flow, becoming an inlet for all there is in God.

I love the story of a mother who despised her son's girlfriend for breaking up with him, which she believed caused him to drink and drive, ultimately perishing in an accident. After many sleepless nights, the boy's mother realized this girl needed more love than hate and phoned the girl to offer her forgiveness. They developed a relationship that has stood the test of time.

> Agape love is described best in Corinthians 13:1-6 (NIV)
>
> If I speak in the tongues of men and angels but have not love, I am only a resounding gong or a clanging cymbal. If I have the gift of prophecy and can fathom all mysteries and all knowledge, and if I have faith that can move mountains but have not love, I am nothing. If I give all my possessions to the poor and surrender my body to the flames but have not love, I gain nothing. Love is patient; love is kind. It does not envy; it does not boast; it is not proud. It is not rude; it is not self-seeking; it is not easily angered and keeps no record of wrongs.

Whenever we manage to love in this capacity, we experience a little slice of heaven right here on earth. As a member of The Beatles, John Lennon wrote "All You Need Is Love," which sums up our practice in five easy-to-understand words. A physician, while giving a talk, claimed the best medicine for any illness is love. An audience member shouted out, "But what if love doesn't work?" He smiled and said, "Just increase the dosage."

# 22

# THE AWAKENING

WHAT IS THE GREATEST OBSTACLE PREVENTING US from experiencing being? In *The Power of Now*, Eckhart Tolle writes, "Identification with your mind," he says, which causes our thoughts to become compulsive. "Not being able to stop thinking is a dreadful affliction, but we do not realize this because almost everybody is suffering from it, so it is considered normal. This incessant mental noise prevents us from finding that realm of inner stillness that is inseparable from being."

There is an old saying that one should sit quietly in meditation for twenty minutes a day unless they are too busy. If this is the case, they will need to meditate for an hour.

It is not easy to overcome the tendency of being trapped by time, rushing through, and resisting everything that comes our way, but it is possible. When asked what he has gained from meditating, the Buddha replied, "Nothing, but let me tell you what I have lost: anger, anxiety, depression, insecurity, and fear of old age and death."

Remember, our thoughts are formative, and if we run around like chickens without heads, we will experience life in this manner. The challenge for us is to silence the mind from its ridiculous overtures and be still. Our souls always know how to heal themselves, but this can be a tricky and sometimes painful process. Khalil Gibran said, "Your pain is the breaking of the shell that encloses your understanding. It is the bitter potion by which the physician within you heals your sick self."

In the book of Isaiah 40:31 (AVS), we read, "They that wait for Jehovah shall renew their strength; they shall mount up with wings as eagles; they shall run and not be weary; they shall walk, and not faint." Many believe meditation is clearing the mind from all thoughts. If this is our goal, most of us will be sadly disappointed.

I believe meditation is the tuning out of our compulsive, egocentric thoughts with almost anything else so we can tune into that still small voice within. I have heard this state of consciousness called Divine Guidance or intuition, both of which work for me.

In 1 Kings 19:11–12 (NIV), we read, "Go out and stand on the mountaintop, for the Lord, your God is about to pass by." It was then that a mighty wind tore into the mountains and shattered the rocks, but God was not in the wind. After the wind, an earthquake, but God was not in the earthquake. After the earthquake, a fire, but God was not in the fire. And after the fire, a still, small voice. Ahh.

The Greek philosopher Epictetus Pititis said, "Let your mind and heart release all that disturbs you. Let your body be still and think of spirit pouring, rushing, and streaming within you and out from you in all directions as you sit quietly." When we reach this level of consciousness, we become an outlet for all there is in God. When we find inner peace, the universe will take notice and act accordingly.

I spoke one day at a neighborhood church on the topic of prayer and meditation. I love talking about this subject, which is often overanalyzed and misunderstood by most of us seeking its benefits. It was a beautiful summer day in New York City. The sun was shining, the birds chirping, the bees were buzzing, and the squirrels were chasing each other as only squirrels can do. It felt good to be alive.

I arrived early and stood by a window overlooking the church's garden as the sky began to darken. A group member came up to share the many ways life was "screwing him over" as massive drops of rain began to fall. A single bumblebee came out of the darkness, flew into one of the window tracks, folded its wings, and became still. I believe this is the objective of meditation; to step out of the storms we experience in life and be still.

I first learned how to meditate by attending services and workshops that included guided meditations as part of the service, but two fifteen-minute segments a week was not cutting it for me. Bugs Bunny once said, "Of course I listen to myself because sometimes I need an expert opinion." For me, and for most of us who are addicted, thinking is a luxury we cannot afford. Remember, it was our best thinking that got us in trouble in the first place.

At a Metro station in Washington DC, a young man with a violin played for about forty-five minutes. People walked through the station, some pausing to drop a few coins into his hat. A toddler stopped and wanted to listen, but his mother pulled him along hurriedly. Several other children wanted to stay, but every parent, without exception, encouraged their children to keep moving. No one noticed, and not one person applauded when he finished playing.

The man wailing on the fiddle was none other than Joshua Bell, one of the greatest violinists we have in the world today. That day he played several pieces from Bach with a violin worth more than $3.5 million. Just two days prior, Joshua sold out a theater in Boston where the average ticket sold for $100 to hear him play the very same music.

Ask yourself this: If we do not have a moment in time to pause and listen to one of the most gifted musicians we have in the world today, what else are we missing out on as we scurry about our days jockeying for a better position in life?

During an exposition of Chinese art, a buyer wanted to purchase a painting depicting a rather barren tree with a few birds sitting on its branches. The woman said to the artist, "I would like to buy this painting, but could you paint in a few more branches?" The artist replied, "Oh no, I couldn't do that; it would not leave enough room for the birds to fly."

There are vast powers of the mind that man has not yet fully developed. Intuition is one of these powers. The American philosopher William James said, "As human beings, we are born with five physical senses, but as spiritual beings, we were born with genius powers that the world little recognizes and rarely uses. Intuition is a faculty of the mind that does not explain but simply points the way."

In 1500 BC Lao Tzu taught, "The human spirit has its source in the divine fountain which must be permitted to flow freely through man." Thus, anyone who flows as life flows has solved the enigma of our existence.

Most people believe prayer is words we offer to God to get Him, Her, or It busy taking care of our business. It is common to hear people say that prayer is talking to God, and meditation is listening for what God's will may be for us. I beg to differ. I believe the sole purpose of meditation is to separate us from our babbling brains so we can be still enough to hear the counsel of our Higher Power. I think prayer then is the practice of that counsel in our everyday lives.

Prayer should not attempt to bend God's will but allow the creative process to do its thing within us. No matter how many words we say, or how loudly we say them, we can never influence God to be anything less than God. We must develop dynamic meditative techniques to prevent the ego from interfering with its flow. We should no longer see prayer as words we speak but something that we are.

In Matthew 6:6 (ESV), Jesus suggested when we pray, we should, "Enter the inner chamber and pray to the Father in secret, as the Father who sees in secret, knows the things you need before you ask." So, the million-dollar question is, why do we ask God for anything?

For some, prayer becomes a never-ending negotiation between God and our egos in a futile attempt to get God to do our will. For anyone already practicing a twelve-step program, I remind you that Step 11 makes this crystal clear. We should pray, "Only for the knowledge of His will for us and the power to carry that out."

In Exodus 3:13–14 (NIV), we read God appeared to Moses in a burning bush, instructing him to return to Egypt and lead the Israelites out of slavery. Moses, described as being about eighty years old and not too keen on the assignment, said to God, Suppose I go to the Israelites and say to them, the God of your fathers has sent me to you, and they ask what his name is? God said to Moses, "I Am that I Am," this is what you are to say to the Israelites. God does not need a name, my friends, only a purpose.

I believe the ministry of Jesus was so compelling because He embodied the practice of affirmative prayer. The two most powerful words ever put together are the great I Am, for what we believe after those words will become our destiny. If you think you cannot, you will not. So if we pray for life, we must be committed to flow as life flows without resistance. Affirm for yourself, I am the hands and face of God, a living expression of love, and God cannot fail.

Throughout the Gospel of John, we read that Jesus affirmed, "I am the light of the world"; "I am the bread of life"; I am the true vine"; "I am the good shepherd"; "I am the way, the truth, and the life." But in Mathew 5:13–14 (NIV), Jesus also affirmed for us, "You are the light of the world." "You are the salt of the earth." We are the ones who will bring light and flavor to an otherwise dark and bland world.

*The Secret*, a book written by Rhonda Byrne, became an international phenomenon. *The Secret* is based on the law of attraction, suggesting our thoughts can directly influence a person's fortunes. For many of us involved in metaphysics for any length of time, *The Secret* was anything but a secret. The law of attraction was taught by Lao Tzu 1,500 hundred years before the ministry of Jesus, by Jesus Himself, and by the many gifted teachers who followed.

Because prayer is so personal to the individual, it would be foolish for me to think I can teach anyone how to pray. But for anyone interested in stepping away from the negotiating table, I want to share with you two prayers and a poem written by Henry Wadsworth Longfellow that I believe holds the essence of prayer and meditation.

# Lakota Prayer

Wakan Tanka, "Great Spirit,"
Teach me how to trust
My heart,
My mind,
My intuition,
My inner knowing,
The senses of my body,
The blessings of my spirit.
Teach me to trust these things
So that I may enter my Sacred Space
And love beyond my fear,
And thus, Walk in Balance
With the passing of each glorious Sun.

# Prayer of St. Francis

Lord, make me an instrument of your peace.
Where there is hatred, let me sow love;
Where there is injury, pardon;
Where there is doubt, faith;
Where there is despair, hope;
Where there is darkness, light;
Where there is sadness, joy.
O Divine Master grant that I may not so much seek
To be consoled as to console,
To be understood as to understand,
To be loved as to love.
For it is in giving that we receive,
It is in pardoning that we are pardoned.

Wikipedia defines synchronicity as "The simultaneous occurrence of events that appear significantly related but have no discernible causal connection." It was Carl Jung who coined the term synchronicity. He wrote, "Whereas some coincidences were without significance, every so often there occurred circumstances so improbable they hinted at a deeper purpose or design."

I always had a passion for getting down and dirty in the streets of whatever city I happened to be in, to be present with our homeless population, which seems to be growing exponentially year after year. One day, my son's friend, Josh, stopped by for me to look at his lower back, which had been bothering him for several weeks. He was curious about why I made so many sandwiches and asked if he could come along for the ride.

I love when others join me to meet, greet, and nourish our outdoor friends, so we grabbed our supplies, got in the car, and began searching the neighborhood for those in need. I usually have a set routine on where I go to be the most productive with my time.

I asked Josh to look up and down the alleys on his side of the street and let me know if he saw anything promising. At one point, he asked me to stop the car as he thought he saw someone who needed our help. Although this area was off my beaten path, I turned the car around anyway and followed Joshua's lead.

Under his direction, we came upon Walter, a seventy-two-year-old Korean War combat veteran of the US Navy. He did not drink, smoke, or do drugs of any kind. This gentleman recently found himself homeless and living on the streets for reasons he did not wish to explain. When asked if he would like one of our food bags, he said he already had something to eat that day and asked us to give it to someone who needed it more than he.

As we were getting ready to leave, I noticed this gentleman's hands and legs were quite swollen. He had pitted edema, tightness in his chest, and difficulty breathing, all symptoms of congestive heart failure. He explained that he went to the VA hospital two days prior but turned away until he could produce two pieces of picture ID.

These, along with most of his possessions, got stolen weeks before while sleeping in the streets.

After making a few well-placed calls, the hospital administrators said we could bring Walter right in. Over a six-day admission, with the help of diuretics, the medical staff drained thirty-two pounds of fluid from his body, which commonly accumulates around the heart and lungs, which can lead to death. This "coincidence" may never have happened if Josh did not injure his back and come along for the ride that day.

One day, a family member asked my advice on what her doctors were calling a postoperative wound infection. This "infection" occurred two days after having a small cyst removed from her groin area. I flew out to manage her care at home. While gathering supplies I would need to treat an infection, a hemostatic agent (used to stop generalized bleeding) must have fallen into the backpack I was taking along with me.

The first time I looked at her wound, it was clear this was not a postoperative infection. It turned out to be a lymphatic gland most likely nicked but not identified at the time of surgery. The milky-looking fluid was coming from beneath a sheath covering the femoral artery and vein. This situation went from being a nuisance to a nightmare overnight. Her doctors were now recommending a vascularized muscle flap, a long and tedious procedure.

When changing her packing, the hemostatic agent I "accidentally" took with me fell out of my backpack and into the pile of supplies I would need for her dressing change. I was unsure if this material would work, but I was confident it would not cause any harm. I packed the material into the wound and added a pressure dressing, which stopped the leak dead in its tracks. This coincidence prevented her from undergoing any additional surgical procedures.

Hospitalized for what ultimately turned out to be a necrotic pulmonary abscess, I developed a DVT (deep vein thrombosis) in my right calf. A year or so later, I bought tickets to fly back to New York to visit my family. Two days before my trip, I developed intense pain and swelling behind my right knee. Concerned this could be another DVT, I called my doctor, who told me to come right in and ordered an ultrasound.

When the doctor returned with my test results (which were not ordered but done bilaterally), he said the DVT in my right leg was old and stable, but I developed a new clot in my left leg, occluding the entire vessel. The pain I was having behind my right knee was due to a ruptured Baker's cyst, painful but not dangerous. The miracle was if I ever boarded that flight to New York, the new clot could have broken off and traveled up to my heart, lungs, or brain, none of which I would favor.

One evening, a world-class swimmer went to practice diving techniques for a competition the following day. The gym was empty; the pool area was dark except for the hint of moonlight flickering through the skylight. Climbing up to the highest board, he extended his arms and took a deep breath. He paused for a moment to pray when a maintenance worker entered the gym and turned on the lights. The swimmer fell to his knees and cried aloud when he saw the pool was empty for repairs.

Let us, then, labor for an inward stillness,
And inward stillness and an inward healing;
That perfect silence where the lips and heart
are still, and we no longer entertain
Our own imperfect thoughts and vain opinions,
But God alone speaks in us, and we wait
In singleness of heart, that we may know
God's will, and in the silence of our spirits,
That we may do God's will, and do that only!
—Henry Wadsworth Longfellow

# 23

# THE GIFT OF A
# GRATEFUL HEART

LOU GEHRIG, NICKNAMED THE IRON HORSE, WAS A Major League Baseball first baseman who played for the New York Yankees from 1923 until 1939. On his thirty-sixth birthday, Gehrig was diagnosed with ALS (amyotrophic lateral sclerosis), the same disease that recently killed world-renowned physicist Stephen Hawking. ALS is a progressive neurological disease affecting the nerve cells in the brain and spinal cord, causing severe muscle atrophy, including the primary muscles used in respiration, eventually leading to death by suffocation.

On July 4, 1939, Gehrig stepped up to the microphones at Yankee Stadium and delivered one of the most iconic speeches in American history. Gehrig bowed his head and said to his devoted fans, "Today I consider myself the luckiest man on the face of the earth. I might have gotten a bad break, but I've got an awful lot to live for."

The sold-out crowd of more than sixty-two thousand stood and applauded for almost two full minutes. As Gehrig stepped back from the microphones, he looked visibly shaken, wiping tears from his eyes. Babe Ruth, Lou's teammate and arguably the greatest baseball player of all time, came over and hugged him as a band played "I Love You Truly," and the crowd chanted, "We love you, Lou." The following day, the *New York Times* called it "One of the most touching scenes ever witnessed on a ball field."

Two years later, Lou Gehrig died of ALS, a disease that would forever be synonymous with his name. The Baseball Writers' Association of America voted Gehrig "the greatest first baseman of all time." A monument in Gehrig's honor currently resides in Yankee Stadium. The Lou Gehrig Memorial Award is given annually to the Major League player who best exhibits Gehrig's integrity.

Although he never played Major League baseball, my vote for this year's Lou Gehrig Award would go to my older brother. He has fought back against lung cancer, brain cancer, three devastating strokes, and is now bedridden with advanced Parkinson's disease.

I cannot remember a single time my brother has ever complained about his lot in life. Although her challenges were somewhat different, my mother was not only a survivor but a perpetual optimist. I thought it was most fitting; my mom took her last breath on a Thanksgiving Day.

Every morning we have a choice of which attitude we will embody throughout the day. Marcus Tullius Cicero said, "Gratitude is not only the greatest of virtues but the parent of all the others." Remember, gratitude, like its counterpart self-pity, is causative energy. What we put out there, we will get back in equal measure. If we start our day with a positive attitude, we will undoubtedly have a better day.

Gratitude is becoming a lost art, especially here in America. Recently, a Brazilian-American friend posted this on her Facebook page: "Whether you like our president or not, distrust our government or not, the salvation for this country is not in the hands of those in power. It is in the hands of those of us who still believe in the power of love."

Life has little to do with what happens to us but how we perceive and act upon those perceptions. By rising above the ego, our self-seeking desires diminish as we tap into the spiritual gift of empathy. There is always someone somewhere facing more significant challenges than us.

If you have seen the inside of a classroom, are in good health, have food to eat, clothes to wear, a roof over your head, and never experienced the horrors of war, you are better off than the million or so who will not survive the week. According to UNICEF, worldwide, more than 1.3 billion children live in extreme poverty, tens of thousands of which will die each day from a lack of food and medicine and the indiscriminate consequences of war.

Fred Rogers, the creator of *Mr. Roger's Neighborhood*, said, "We live in a world in which we need to share responsibility. It is easy to say it is not my child, not my community, not my world, not my problem. Then there are those who see the need and respond. I consider those people my heroes." I bet you never thought a nut job like me would be quoting the likes of Fred Rodgers, but those of us living in Mr. Harrison's neighborhood needed a break from reality every once in a while.

Mahatma Gandhi said, "We must widen the circle of our love until it embraces the whole village. In turn, the village must take into its fold the district, then the district to the province, and so on until the scope of our love encircles the whole world. I have found that the more I care for the happiness and well-being of others, the greater is my sense of well-being."

Whether we label it good or bad, energy circulates from one person to another through a dynamic exchange of ideas and substance. For the law of attraction to manifest the good we desire, we must first understand the law of reciprocity, that giving and receiving are equal partners. It is only through the act of giving that we receive. Thus, the more we share our time, talent, and treasure, the more will flow in our direction without asking God for any favors.

While visiting Washington, I stopped at a gas station to fill my tank when I noticed a five-dollar bill left at the pump. It had a note attached that said, "You are blessed." It was the first time I was ever on the receiving end of a random act of kindness like this. Although I did not need the money, I took it anyway, believing there was a higher purpose for it I did not yet understand.

On returning home, a Brazilian couple was visiting with their two boys, ages eight and ten. As they were getting ready to leave, I handed the boys twenty-dollar bills and instructed them to spend the money on anything they wanted.

But, if they chose to give the money to charity, I would double the amount. The parents quickly picked up on the idea and offered to do the same. That day $120 was donated to an orphanage in Brazil, all because of one small random act of kindness.

Unfortunately, I have also experienced the unsettling effects of not seizing the opportunity to give. While standing in an extraordinarily long line at the DMV, I heard a representative tell a woman she needed three additional dollars to complete her transaction. The woman, who had two young children with her and one on the way, said she had the money out in her car and would have to run out to get it. Although I had extra cash in my pocket, I stood there like an idiot and did nothing.

While folding clothes in a local laundromat, I watched as a homeless man picked up an empty plastic bottle and attempted to throw it into a commercial recycling bin on a particularly windy day. It took several attempts before the bottle stayed within the container. Later in the day, I ran into this gentleman and asked why he spent so much time trying to get that one plastic bottle into the bin. He said, "We all got to do whatever we can do to help."

I love the story of the young lady walking along the shoreline, throwing starfish that washed up with the high tide back into the sea. A local beachcomber stopped and asked the girl, "Do you not realize there are thousands of starfish lying on this beach? You cannot possibly make a difference."

The girl picked up another starfish, threw it back into the ocean, and said, "I believe it made a difference to that one." The Dalai Lama quipped, "If you think you are too small to make a difference, try sleeping with a mosquito."

When we have an opportunity to give, we should do so before the ego gets involved, for it has the power to override our hearts, convincing us we do not have enough time or money to fill the need. But giving is not found in our wallets, nor counted in time, but is the out-picturing of a grateful heart.

I believe there are a few elements in the art of giving that must be incorporated into our practice of giving if we wish to reap its benefits.

First, when we have something to offer, we provide it without preconditions or expectations. One evening one of our outdoor friends asked me to purchase a hot dog for her with double mac and cheese from a street vendor that charged me the tourist price of $5.75. When we sat down to eat, she picked at the mac and cheese, then got up and threw the entire hot dog, bun, and all into the trash. She said she was only interested in eating the toppings. God has quite a sense of humor, wouldn't you say?

Secondly, when we give, we must not seek the recognition of others. If we do, our egos may get stroked, but we strike out in our efforts to improve our conscious contact with the God of our understanding.

There were years where I made a ridiculous amount of money, both at work and in the stock market. Neighborhood friends, strapped for cash, needed to obtain an MRI of their son's brain. A mutual friend was collecting money to raise the $1,200 required for the study.

As my wife and I will be forever grateful our children were born healthy, we wrote a check for $1,000 with instructions that our donation remain anonymous. Unfortunately, the word got out, and we received accolades from many of our neighbors, including the couple to whom we donated the money.

I have been on both sides of the fence with this one, and I can tell you when I give to be recognized, I always come up empty. It is only when my ego remains out of the process of giving; I feel God's presence in the act of my giving. I also believe our giving should be in proportion to what we have received, and it should sting a little.

At most meetings I attend, we pass a basket around for those members who can financially support the group. During the collection, I often think of the biblical account of when a widow put what amounted to a few pennies in the temple's treasury. Speaking to His disciples, Jesus said, "This poor widow put in more than all the other contributors. They have contributed from their surplus, but she, from her poverty."

When visiting Brazil, my son and I took daily walks to the beach, purchased fresh coconuts, and drank the chilled water (*água de côco*) down by the shore. One afternoon, as we walked to the beach, we came across a scene that will be etched in my memory forever.

A middle-aged man covered in dirt from head to toe was in the street, begging for something to eat from local shop owners who kept shoo-shooing him away. Although the man had a horse-drawn carriage nearby, there was no horse attached to it. We watched as the man strapped a harness over his shoulders and struggled to get the wheels to engage.

My son turned to me and asked if there was something we could do to help.

Unfortunately, the only cash I had with me was the two dollars I stuffed in my bathing suit to purchase the coconuts. I told my son it was his choice; he could offer the money to the man, but we would have to abandon our coconut run for the day. I felt a great sense of pride on that day, as my son chose compassion over selfishness.

I want to share a couple of stories about gifts I received that money cannot buy. Toward the end of one of our sacred circle groups, in which I was a facilitator, a member handed me a thank you note with an original photograph of Mother Teresa on her knees praying in a small church in Calcutta.

She wrote, "This is one of my most cherished possessions. May it be a blessing in your life. You have a wonderful gift to share. Your holy name is Jyotish, which in Sanskrit means the bringer of life."

The second story centers around a six-string guitar I received as a Christmas gift about thirty-five years ago. The guitar, made of cardboard and twine, was put together by two of my nieces, ages six and nine, whose parents were in the middle of a contentious divorce.

A lot of thought and an abundance of love went into the making of that guitar. I kept it in a prominent place in my living room for more than six years until it finally disintegrated. The guitar may be long gone, but I will never forget the love of those who made it for me.

A senior who recently lost his wife after sixty-four years of marriage sat in his backyard sobbing. His next-door neighbors were a single mom and a four-year-old boy. When they returned home from an outing, the boy asked his mother if he could go over to comfort the man. The mother said he could, and off he went.

Ten minutes later, the mother peeked through the bushes to see the boy sitting in the man's lap, who was now laughing. During dinner, the mom asked the boy what he said to make their neighbor feel better. Her son replied, "I did not say anything, Mommy. I just sat in his lap and helped him cry."

I learned a valuable lesson from my father, who drank for more than fifty-seven years but remained alcohol-free for the last year of his life. Nobody is too old or too sick to recover from the devastating effects of this disease. Although I believe any addict seeking recovery can find it, some will remain hellbent on destroying themselves no matter what.

A few years ago, I flew back to New York to help a childhood friend I shot dope with to become open to the possibility of getting clean. After attending half a dozen meetings with me, my friend said, "I cannot do this, Sean, it's too scary."

I told him I understood and did the only thing I could do. I packed my bags and went back home. If I admit I am powerless over my addiction, I most certainly have no power over another's self-destructive behaviors.

East Coast, West Coast, and all around the town, this disease is relentless in its pursuit of increasing its body count whenever possible. A friend who was in and out of recovery for many years died after being taken into police custody. The officers responded to reports of an intoxicated man running naked in and out of traffic in downtown San Diego. This time was not the first time he demonstrated this type of behavior after relapsing.

After being handcuffed, he continued struggling with the officers. At some point, a spokesman for the police department said he went into "medical distress" and taken by ambulance to the hospital. He was pronounced dead shortly before midnight. An autopsy report is still pending, but for this addict, it matters not. Here today, gone tomorrow; it is the nature of the beast.

Helping others, especially those who are addicted and homeless, can be frustrating and sometimes downright dangerous, but this work is always gratifying and, at times, a whole lot of fun. Do you remember the story I told in the previous chapter where my son's friend Josh became the hero by which Walter, a homeless Korean War veteran, got to live another day?

Well, Josh called this a transformational event and called his parents on the East Coast to tell them about his experience. A few months later, Joshua's parents came to San Diego to visit their son and wanted to meet me. I invited their family over to my place at the beach for an early evening barbeque.

As my guest arrived earlier than expected, I asked everyone to go down to the beach until I finished cooking. I wanted to be fully present during our conversations. When I walked down to let them know the food was ready, I met one of our outdoor friends who I never had the pleasure of meeting before. He said his name was General Lee, who, at the time, was having a frank discussion with his nemesis, General Grant.

I asked the general if he would be our guest of honor at the barbeque. He took me up on my offer and followed me home. I introduced him to our guests on the balcony and went inside to make his plate.

When we sat down to eat, the general apologized, for one hour earlier, he took a hit of ecstasy and was no longer hungry. I believed Joshua's parents might have been a little apprehensive at first, but to their credit, they went with the flow.

When asked if I regretted inviting General Lee over when meeting Josh's parents for the first time, my answer was a resounding no. Remember, his parents were here to support the work I do on behalf of the homeless. By the time dinner was over, my guests all seemed to be enjoying each other's company—some by overcoming their misperceptions about the homeless and General Lee via a little synthetic pill called ecstasy.

There are as many ways to give as people are willing to give. I believe the one essential element in the art of giving is that our gifts come from a grateful heart. Our gratitude must speak for us out in the community. It only takes a smile or a few kind words to brighten up someone else's day. Whatever our social or economic status may be, we can always be kind.

# 24

# BREAKING THE CHAINS
# OF ADDICTION

I DID NOT WRITE THIS BOOK TO SEEK AN ADDITIONAL platform to preach to my fellow addicts, who already found their way into recovery. My purpose is to help those individuals whose lives have been flipped upside down by the recent opioid epidemic now playing in small-town theaters everywhere. I want to speak directly to the parents of addicted children who are overwhelmed and ill-equipped to deal with the complexities of this disease.

Whether children carry a specific gene associated with addiction or not, they are but a pile of clay waiting to be molded by those around them. An infant is born innocent and knows nothing of hatred, prejudice, and intolerance toward others. These character traits, just like love, compassion, and empathy, are not passed down from generation to generation via any specific genetic code but are instilled in us by our exposure to them.

I love the story about a concerned mother who went to see the Buddha as her son became addicted to sugar. After listening to her plea, the Buddha told the mother to come back three days later for his counsel. When the mother returned with her wayward son, the Buddha addressed the boy directly and said, "Listen to your mother and stop eating sugar."

Although appreciative of his decision, the mother asked why they needed to wait three long days for such a simple response. The Buddha explained, "Before I could tell your son to stop eating sugar, I needed to stop eating it myself." The most effective way for us to help others is by being a living example of that which is possible.

Would it not be wiser to spend a little extra time building healthy-minded, self-assured children than wasting a lifetime trying to repair a broken adult? Ann Landers said, "It's not what you do for your children, but what you have taught them to do for themselves, that will make them successful human beings. Children need to learn to take responsibility for their actions, so they don't become adults believing that nothing is ever their fault."

In *The Prophet,* Khalil Gibran writes, "Your children are not your children. They are the sons and daughters of life's longing for itself. They come through you but not from you, and though they are with you, yet they belong not to you. You may give them your love, but not your thoughts, for they have their own thoughts."

Gibran continues, "You may house their bodies but not their souls, for their souls' dwell in the house of tomorrow, which you cannot visit, not even in your dreams. You may strive to be like them but seek not to make them like you. For life goes not backward, nor tarries with yesterday."

The American bald eagle is known to build the most extensive chick-friendly nests for its offspring. When her fledglings are ready to leave the nest, the mother eagle will begin removing all the soft material she built into its lining, making it progressively more uncomfortable for them to stay. If the chicks do not leave voluntarily, she will nudge them over the edge. There is a universal conspiracy in place that insists life keeps moving forward.

Next to marriage (or being in any committed relationship), raising children has to be the most challenging thing we do. Every child is different, and there has never been a book written or roadmap designed to help parents raise happy, healthy, and productive members of our society. However, there have been many studies on what children will require as adults to make it out in the real world.

*All I Really Need to Know I Learned in Kindergarten,* written by Robert Fulghum, outlines fundamental lessons of life most of us learn in kindergarten but have long since forgotten. It explains how the world would be a better place if adults adhered to the same basic rules as children: be kind to one another, share, do not take things that do not belong to you, clean up your mess, play fair, flush, and always wash your hands before you eat.

As a kid, I learned to be quiet and listen when adults were speaking to me. To say yes or no, sir or ma'am, when asked a question. To answer, please, and thank you when appropriate. Hold doors open for those walking behind me. To give up my seat while riding public transportation to all women, the elderly, and anyone appearing disabled in any way. Believe it or not, most of these practices, no matter how strung out I was, stayed with me throughout my active addiction and remain in place today.

One-way we parents can help our children avoid the maladapted personality traits associated with addiction is not to push them to be exceptional in any way but help them see the beauty, joy, and wonder in the ordinary. When we pressure our children to be what they are not, they tend to become adult perfectionists, moving throughout life, berating themselves how they could have and should have done better.

Just as there are no perfect children, there are no perfect parents. Not all parents are the causative agents if their kids become chemically dependent. I know of good parents whose children are addicted and vice versa. I believe we can stack the deck in our favor, however, by not only criticizing our children when they could have done better but praise them equally when they have done their best.

When our son Jason was born, he suffered from chronic ear infections, a significant tongue thrust, and was the second child in a bilingual household, all of which made it more challenging for him to learn. After getting through preschool, kindergarten, and first grade, my wife and I were concerned about his ability to keep up academically. His doctor explained, "Because of his recurrent ear infections, Jason's hearing was like the way we hear when submerged underwater."

While attending Jason's fourth-grade parent/teacher conference, his teacher told us how well he was doing this year. As we wiped tears of joy off our faces, the teacher must have thought we were getting upset. She said, "Oh no, don't worry; Jason is right in the middle of the pack." I explained that hearing the words "in the middle" regarding our son's ability to learn was music to our ears.

My son and daughter have always believed I favored the other, so I must be doing something right. Sibling rivalry is a phenomenon essential for creating long-lasting bonds between siblings, thus strengthening the whole family unit. It is a thing called mother nature and is prevalent throughout the animal kingdom.

My wife, son, and daughter are also black belts in Tae Kwon Do. Our involvement in the martial arts came when, in the sixth grade, Jason was again having difficulty paying attention. There was a suggestion by some that he was showing signs of ADD and might do well with a new "miracle drug" called Adderall.

My wife and I were conflicted about the idea of medicating our son at such an early age. We were delighted when we heard from other parents that Tae Kwon Do help their children stay focused without medication. I am happy to report it worked for us as well.

Our son towered over his older sister in their teens and believed he no longer had to "suck up" and obey her commands. This shift was the beginning of an ongoing war of the minds, as our daughter may have been smaller in stature but was born a giant. She is self-motivated, self-assured, self-reliant, and not afraid to speak up for herself. Our daughter was the "capo de capo" (boss of all bosses) in our family.

While in the kitchen preparing something to eat, the kids returned from school more animated than usual, engaged in dueling monologs, which one was smarter, classier, and of course, "hotter" than the other. As my daughter walked past my son, he poked her in the back of her ribs. Without any indication of what was about to happen, she turned around and executed a perfectly placed roundhouse kick to the left side of her brother's head. Pow!

I did not condone the use of violence inside or outside our home unless physically threatened by another. After strongly admonishing my daughter for her temporary lapse of judgment, I turned around and found myself smiling. It was apparent the only damage sustained in this encounter was to my son's ego. As a dad, I was proud of my daughter. She reacted how every martial artist trains to respond when attacked from behind.

Children today may do well academically, can maneuver around the internet, and have hundreds of friends on social media but cannot engage in meaningful conversation with anyone. Recently, I passed a group of teenagers sitting at a table outside a fast-food restaurant. Each was self-absorbed in their electronic devices as if no one else was sitting at the table. How will this e-generation ever function in a world build on interpersonal relationships when the only way to develop them is by participating in them?

While our kids were still in high school, we attended a charity event for special needs children. I bid on and won dinner for four at a restaurant in downtown San Diego hosted by two-time Olympic gold medal winner, Monique Henderson. Who better to teach our children what it takes to be successful than an Olympic champion? This incredible experience costs less in donations than the price of a semester in college for one of our kids.

Our daughter invited us to attend her final examination to complete her business degree in college. There were bonus points given if the student's parents came to observe the class. Her professor explained this would be an oral examination as he believed written tests are worthless out in the real world. He added, "I want to see if the students are capable of handling the pressure that is endemic in boardroom meetings."

I believe we, the parents, were invited to maximize the pressure put on the students. I felt more tension sitting in this classroom than at any time working in the operating room. It was like watching a game of Jeopardy at warp speed. The professor shouted out questions, and if the student hesitated or tried to make something up, he would deduct any number of points from their total. Toward the end, he told one of the students not to bother answering any more questions. He would have to repeat the course.

Not my favorite, but one of the more influential teachers I ever had was the Surgical Director of my program. As we began our rotations, our director assigned my classmates to smaller procedures like hernia repairs, tonsillectomies, vein stripping, and breast biopsies. My first case was on a thoracolumbar scoliosis reduction with Harrington rods, which took seven hours to complete.

On graduation day, I asked our director why she assigned me to some of the most complicated procedures that filtered into the operating room. She said, "It was because I liked you, Sean. I knew if I could get you to do big cases like these as a student, you would never shy away from them throughout your career." We should all be so lucky to have teachers such as these.

Throughout grade school, the kids in my neighborhood referred to me as the "mean daddy" on the block. As my son would tell me years later, "None of the other dads ever called the police on his kids." My son did not realize the officer who came to visit was a good friend who worked with juveniles for the courts but was not there in any official capacity.

If I came across a group of our neighborhood kids hanging out in the canyon, where they were not supposed to be, I would question them separately (with their parents' blessings) and say, "You only have this one opportunity. If you tell me the truth, I will not tell your parents what you were doing. If not, you are on your own."

I always kept my word, and the trust I built with these kids came in handy years later when they started driving and were exposed to drugs and alcohol. We made it clear to our kids if they, or any of their friends, drank or smoked too much, we would pick them up and bring them home, no questions asked. I was grateful when, on several occasions, we had the opportunity of doing just that.

For the most part, I gave my kids the flexibility to make many of their own decisions, and thus, their own mistakes, holding them accountable when warranted. Out of the many examples I could give, this one came at the expense of my son, in whom I am well pleased. The lesson had to do with when you are in a group, though your hands may not get dirty, you are equally responsible for the group's misdeeds.

The summer before high school began, I was stunned to receive a call from the mother of one of Jason's classmates. She said Jason and a few of his friends left several messages on their answering machine intended for their thirteen-year-old daughter.

These messages ranged from rude to vulgar to vile. I listened to the recordings, and although my son's voice was not on any of them, I asked the father of the young lady, who happened to be the football coach of the high school Jason was about to attend if he would help me teach my son a lesson.

We planned to have him come over a week later to offer his apology, giving Jason time to think of what it would be like to meet his freshman football coach under these circumstances. Approaching D-Day, Jason became less and less confident in his ability to weather the storm. As we drove over to the coach's house that day, his anxiety level was palpable.

When we arrived, the mother, daughter, and the father, who looked like a linebacker himself, were standing in the foyer waiting for us. After introductions, I asked if we could all listen to the messages together. I believe in the awkwardness of the moment

Jason developed a smirk on his face, so I asked, "Do you think this is funny?"

I turned to the girl's father and said, "I am going to wait outside, let me know when you're finished with him," and walked out. It was not part of the plan, but I think my little hissy fit worked to set the stage for my son's one-on-one meeting with the coach. And coach he did. That day my son learned about the power of forgiveness and what it takes to be a man.

Although tempting, I never felt the need to invade my children's privacy by reading their texts, emails, or social media posts. I wanted to develop a relationship with them built on honesty and mutual respect. I would say to them, "Good kids get?" They would respond by saying, "Good things." I would then say, "Bad kids get?" They would respond by saying, "Nothing." Even as adults, they still respond to my questions the same way they did twenty years ago. So cute!

My children may get a little neurotic at times, but I believe they have done well for themselves because they learned some of these tough life-lessons early on. Whenever my son, now twenty-eight, and I sleep under the same roof, I still tuck him in at night, letting him know how much I love him. I went from being called the mean daddy by the kids on our block to earn the title "Pappi Homie, the Goat," father of the homeboys, the greatest of all times.

# 25

# TO BEE OR NOT TO BEE

D R. ELIZABETH KUBLER-ROSS, A PIONEER IN NEAR-death studies and author of *On Death and Dying*, wrote, "The most beautiful people we have ever known are those who have known defeat, known suffering, known struggles, known loss, and have found their way out of the depths of despair."

After being struck and paralyzed by a drunk driver in 1989, Danielle Stento wrote, "Sometimes the things that seem to hurt us the most are the very things that bring out the best in us. They are the struggles that help us discover the faith we thought we lost, the strength we did not know we had, and the courage to let go of the past and begin again. Because challenges help us see who we are, where we want to go, and what our lives can be if only we have faith and keep on trying."

We must remember no one will be beaming down from the Starship Enterprise to rescue us from the inner demons we alone created in the first place. It takes vigilance and a lifelong commitment to co-create a new way of being with our higher selves, aligning it with the infinite power of love. From the Cherokee tradition, we hear, "The path of the warrior is lifelong, and mastery is often achieved simply by staying on the path."

Sooner or later, we all come to a place on our spiritual path, where we experience a "dark night of the soul." At different times throughout her life, Mother Teresa questioned the very existence of God. Stay awake, my friends, for if this could happen to a devoted soul like Mother Teresa, do I need to say more?

The broken-window theory studies the norm-setting effect on additional crimes and antisocial behavior in economically depressed neighborhoods. It proposes monitoring fractured urban environments to prevent such crimes as petty theft, vandalism, and public intoxication. In turn, this will help create an atmosphere of law and order, thereby preventing more serious crimes from occurring. For those wishing to find ongoing recovery, this theory has proven invaluable. Not only should we seek out those character defects that are currently making our lives unmanageable, but the more subtle ones before they turn into monsters.

Life for us becomes a projection of the thoughts we have and the choices we make. No matter what obstacles we may encounter, we must try to keep moving forward. However, like Yoda wisely counseled the young Luke Skywalker, "Try not. Do or do not. There is no try."

Von Goethe asked, "Are you in earnest? Seize this very moment. Whatever you can do or dream you can do, begin it. Boldness has genius, power, and magic in it." No sooner are words like these said when the ego takes center stage and declares, "Wow, that sounds great; let's start tomorrow." But sometimes there is no next time; tomorrow may never come.

Teddy Roosevelt said, "Do what you can, with what you have, right where you are."

St. Francis suggests we start our days by doing what is necessary, then what is possible, and suddenly we are doing the impossible. The word impossible will have no power over those who have come to trust in the process.

It would behoove us to stay far away from those "friends" who seem to have problems with every solution. There comes a time when we know we need to step away from the drama we co-created with others. Life is too short to be anything but happy.

I love the thoughts of Abraham Lincoln, the sixteenth president of the United States. When questioned about his cheerful attitude on a day, thousands of soldiers under his command died on the battlefield, Lincoln quipped, "A man is about as happy as he makes up his mind to be."

Two monks were returning to the monastery after a long night of prayer and meditation. It rained throughout the day, leaving deep puddles of muddy water on the roads. They came upon a woman trapped by a fast-moving stream. The elder picked the woman up and carried her across to the other side of the road.

As the monks continued walking, the younger berated the elder. Indignant, he said, "Sir, as monks, we cannot touch a woman." The elder acknowledged the words he spoke were of truth. He then asked, "But sir, how is it then that you picked that woman up and carried her across the road?"

The elder monk finally had enough and said, "I picked the woman up but promptly put her down. It appears to me you are still carrying her."

I sat across the counter from a bank teller who was visibly upset. The previous night someone keyed her new sports car. As we worked on my transaction, my son called from Madrid, where he was doing an internship to finish his business degree. A bunch of locals jumped him in a downtown night club. He said he got hit a couple of times but was doing okay. The next words out of his mouth were, "Dad; I got to go; they're coming back." I told him to call me when it was safe to do so and hung up the phone.

I apologized to the young lady for the disruption and asked if I needed to sign anything before leaving. She looked bewildered and asked, "Did that just really happen, or was it a joke?" When I assured her the call was in real-time, she asked, "Why then are you not more concerned?"

I said to her, "By the time I could do anything to help my son, who is in a foreign land thousands of miles away, the incident would be long over. The only logical thing I could do is wait for him to call back."

On the night of December 9, 1914, Thomas Edison watched his life's work go up in smoke when his laboratory in Orange, New Jersey, burned to the ground. While walking upon the charred ruins, Edison said, "There is great value in disaster. The fire consumed all our previous mistakes; thank God we can start anew." He promised to rebuild, and in three weeks, Edison's company released the first phonograph, allowing us to listen to the music of our choosing in the comfort of our homes.

I had the honor of sitting down and talking with former heavyweight boxing champion Floyd Patterson, "The Gentleman Boxer," over dinner one evening. There was a combination of medical personnel, boxing enthusiasts, and a local news crew sitting at the table. I was seated directly across from the champ, so we talked for quite a while. After dinner, the reporter came over with cameras rolling.

During the interview, the reporter brought up Patterson's statistics, which included sixty-four fights with fifty-five wins, forty by knock out. He also brought up the fact that Floyd held the record for being knocked down more than any other boxer in heavyweight history.

The champ responded by saying, "Well, if I hold the record for being knocked down the most, I must also hold the record for getting up, as I never stayed down for the count."

Our progress should not be measured by how often we get knocked down but by how we bounce back from adversity. Success is a natural byproduct that occurs when these spiritual practices become a way of life. Yes, life is tough, and we will inevitably encounter obstacles along the way. But these are the ties that bind our dreams together, making us more determined to succeed.

So how rich do you think you are? One man said, "I think I've done well in life, I started with nothing, and I still have it." Others are so poor, the only thing they have is money. This gentleman has not accumulated much in worldly possessions, but he is the owner of a grateful heart. He possesses the love of family and friends. This man may not appear wealthy by human standards but is rich beyond measure.

Actor Jim Carrey said, "I think everybody should get rich and famous so they could see that money is not the answer."

I have heard Michael Beckwith, a Unity friend and founder of the Agape International Spiritual Center in Culver City, say, "Money has become our God and accumulation has become our practice." Money itself is not evil, my friends. It is our addiction to money that corrupts our souls.

No one has it all figured out, and pretending we do does not make us appear smarter but self-centered, insecure, and untrustworthy in others' eyes. No one likes a know-it-all. It is our vulnerability that connects us with others and puts them at ease to express themselves freely.

A neighbor posted this on her Facebook page, "I just had a one-hour argument with one of my clients over sausage links. I can't do this job anymore." Finding humor in life's many struggles is one of the best tools we have for stopping the ego from wallowing in self-pity.

One morning, a woman looked in the mirror and noticed she only had three hairs on her head. "Well," she said, "I think I will braid my hair today." She did so and had a good day.

The next morning, she looked in the mirror and saw she only had two strands left. "Well," she said, "I think I will part my hair down the middle today." She did so and had a great day.

The next morning she looked in the mirror and noticed she had only one hair left. "Well," she said, "Today, I am going to wear my hair in a ponytail." She did so and had a great day.

The next morning, she looked in the mirror and noticed she had no hair left on her head. "Yeah!" she shouted. "I don't have to fix my hair at all today."

Wouldn't it be great if we could live our lives in this manner, accepting life on life's terms, unafraid of the judgments of others?

The fight against aging, like the fight against addiction, is a battle nobody can win. Once again, we must surrender to our reality or suffer the consequences. We should never allow ourselves to grow old, no matter how long we live. Life is precious, and we must make a conscious effort to remember each day is a gift.

Let us stop thinking about degenerating and appreciate the time we have left by living our lives from within, the only place we can remain forever young. Recently, I received a coupon in the mail entitling me to be cremated free of charge. Unfortunately, this offer came without any of the bells and whistles I would like to have with me during my incineration. On the back, there was an expiration date of September 2022. Do you think they know something I do not?

Remember, we are never alone in our struggles. Someone somewhere is going through similar challenges. In Hinduism, we often see the word Namaste; "I honor the place in you in which the whole universe dwells. I honor the place in you that is of love, light, truth, and peace. When you are in that place in you, and I am in that place in me, we are one."

Chief Seattle said, "Humankind has not woven the web of life. We are but one thread within it. Whatever we do to the web, we do to ourselves. All things are bound together; all things connect." Everything we have, including time, is borrowed. There is no mine, only ours. I heard of an Indian tribe that considers how their decisions will affect the tribe for the next seven generations to come.

If we have but only one prayer, let it be that we stay centered and balanced so nothing can disturb our inner peace. Let us not dwell on our past mistakes but press on to the higher calling of God. Let us be enthusiastic about our future, rejoice in others' success, and live-in peace with God and all his children.

In Genesis 19 (NIV), we read angels spoke to Lot and said, "Hurry, take your wife and daughters and flee for your lives! Flee to the mountains and never look back." Lot, always trying to negotiate his way out of trouble, said, "No, my Lord. You have shown me great kindness in sparing my life, but look, there is a small town nearby, let us flee to it." The angels said to him, "Very well, we will grant this request, but escape quickly, for the cities of Sodom and Gomorrah are about to be destroyed."

The story told is that as God rained down fire and brimstone over the cities of Sodom and Gomorrah, Lot's wife became curious about the life she left behind. Forgetting or unwilling to take her angel's advice, she looked back and turned into a pillar of salt.

For me, there is no turning back. Finally, after all these years, I feel perfectly content, and I will not let any of the puppet masters or my ego take that away from me.

In *Walden,* Henry David Thoreau writes, "If one advances confidently in the direction of his dreams and endeavors to live the life he has imagined, he will meet with a success unexpected in common hours. He will pass an invisible boundary; new, universal, and more liberal laws will begin to establish themselves around and within him. He will live with the license of a higher order of being."

If we wish to experience "heaven" right here on earth, we must never again see ourselves as victims of our past or slaves to the meaningless. We must rise above the ego's perceptions and judgments and live in communion with our higher selves. The secret of having a happy life is letting things unfold in their natural way until we have taken our very last breath. As the writer knows, it is not the first but the final chapter of our lives that will show us how well we ran the race.

# 26

# MUSIC MAGIC
# LYRICS AND LOVE

**(All songs written between 1987- 1989)**

## "Multiple"

I'm locked in a closet; Mommy, I'm scared.
There are mice all around me; it's dark in here.
You put me in the closet, and I don't have the key.
Mommy, Mommy, Mommy, why you do this to me?

Doctor, Doctor, Doctor, can you help me, please?
I am forever changing people; who's the real me?
My friends all left me; they don't understand,
the complicated life of a multiple man.

I'm a multiple; I got people in me; I'm a multiple personality.
Talking via people I develop in me; I'm a multiple personality.

Greetings from the seven brothers, greetings from the little boy,
Greetings from the avid homo, I am the one who feels the joy.
Greetings from the seven no ones,
Greetings from the splintered man.

Listen, people of the earth, tell me it's true.
I'm not into para; there are people and you.
Let me snap my fingers and count to ten.
One by one, I'll bring us out again.

## "Forum"

I'm a drug-infested boy.
It's a fantasy reality.
I like the devil's little joys.
It's the girls with horns upon their heads for me.

I'm a masturbator,
the uni-kind of sexuality.
And I'm a demonstrator,
So let me demonstrate myself to you tonight.

They call me paranoid-schizoid—
You're doing this, but you're saying that—
And my body starts to twitch.
These are the things I offer you tonight.

I'm a drug-infested boy,
I'm a drug-infested boy,
I'm a drug-infested boy.
Well, I'm just a boy.

## "Dancing in the Valley of Sin"

Looking for somewhere to begin, I feel like dancing.
Dancing with you under my gun.
Look at me, I'm having such fun, you keep me dancing.
I got your number—A-number one.

Every time I look in your eyes, I see a fire.
Got to get it out from within.
Looking for somewhere to begin, you feel like dancing,
Dancing in the Valley of Sin.

Let's dance, just pick your feet up, dance, dance, dance.
Let's dance, just let your body talk, dance, dance, dance.

A thing is coming out of my head, I got that feeling.
Got to get it closer to you.
I want to love you till you turn blue;
I love to please you.
Pleasing me is part of that too.

Looking for somewhere to begin, I can't believe it.
They're telling me this love is a lie.
Look at you: you move like spies for your romancing,
Your dancing in the Valley of Sin.

## "Vapor"

Listen to me, children; I know what I say.
If you ever had that feeling, you're fading away.
Life is just a bummer, a mainline to pain.
Snorting little white lies, you're fading away.

Dancing in a corner, with nobody but you.
Your mommy died early; your father's gone too.
You bore a bastard baby and wished he turned blue.
You're just another vapor; you're fading away.

It's true; you're breaking my heart in two, burning your brain!

Open the windows, the eyes to the mind.
Try to find a feeling, somewhere inside.
I came to light your dark life; you'd rather be blind.
You treat my love like garbage; you throw it away.

You hold clandestine virtues, like peas in a pod.
Temporary guilt trips, thinking of God.
Don't want to face your problems; you live in a maze.
Just like the leaves in autumn, you're blowing away.

## "No Talk Ease"

Hey lady, you're a natural.
Just maybe you got it all.
Pure art form, your eyes shine on me,
But you're talking, no talk ease.

Hey, lady, ala motion,
I want to swimma in your ocean.
I'm loaded and aimed to please,
But you're talking, no talk ease.

I'm going to find a home …
I'm going to find a home …
I thought I belonged here!

Hey guys, the girls are animals!
It's a thing called mother nature.
Hey girls, you're all animals—
But remember, it's a man's world.

Hey lady, what are you doing?
Don't think that you're a shoe-in.
I found out; you talk the tease,
with your talking, no talk ease.

## "Out of the Blue"

You're a neonate, a creature of the new.
You're a neonate, so what're you going to do to change my world?
You came out of the blue; you were sent here by the gods to change
my world.

Full of life, you're like the Talking Heads.
You fill my mind as I'm lying here in bed.
I think of you, you fill my world.
You came out of the blue; you were sent here by the gods to change
my world.

As I see her, I keep holding on, holding on, holding on.
Hold it; she's a vapor. She fades away, fades away, fades away,
She disappears into her lonely life, lonely nights, lonely days too.

Well, they call you Trish, but your mommy named you Pat.
If I can make a wish, you know I'm wishing that you'll be my girl,
you'll be my world.
You came out of the blue; you were sent here by the gods to change
my world.

## "Life in Pittsburgh"

I wake up Monday morning; you're coming into view.
We talked last night by tele, exchanging points of view.
I see you in the moonlight, dancing to Talking Heads.
I am really a kind of shy guy; I want you, but I run instead.

I'm visiting Pittsburgh, a ménage à trois crusade.
This city's full of youngblood, pumping hot—I am ready to stay.
The lights are flashing heaven, but I'm dancing deep in hell.
I thought you met my eyeballs, but you met his lies as well.

But I came to see you, I did not run away.
You must be something special—what else can I say?

I will not see the shadows; I will not feel the rain.
I count my dreams and hours, fly as high as planes.
My prayers are said in colors, there is more to life than gray.
I know I'll find that lover to like my every way.
I came to see you!

## "9.5"

This generation's crazy—what's up, Doc?
Instead of just a person, they think I'm a not.
The girls are scary monsters; they come up from the sea.
Just like a mean Godzilla, they vaporize me.

The facts are there beside me; I cannot run away.
The women of the '80s—they're gonna kill me someday.
They put me in an oven; I'm overdone.
This is the way most women like to have fun.

The other girls I know, they don't give a damn
About the little pleasures I like as a man.
Thinking of themselves; there's nothing left for me.
If I put them on a scale, they measure zero to three.

But you're a 9.5 on the Richter scale.
You shake me, shake me, shake me like a tree.
You're a 9.5 on the Richter scale, you open the very core of me.

I think you're kind of special, you say you like my mind.
You like to look inside me; we are two of a kind.
Running from the shadows, we both know who we are.
I'm your knight in shining armor; you are my brightest star.

## "The City of Life"

I am surviving, I am depressed.
It's part of life-ing; forget the rest.
As a young boy, I was depressed.
Not always conscious, this world a test.

We're told there is a heaven,
We're told there is a light.
In every heart of man,
there's a city of life.

I'm on vacation; I need a rest.
In my own mind, I like it best.
I am creative; I love the earth.
I see in God's eyes a new rebirth.

I'm feeling godly; I'm into God,
from Christ to Buddha, Horus to Rah,
I am surviving the holy test.
Bring on the life-ing, cheer on my death.

I am surviving …
I am surviving …
I am surviving—
I am depressed.

## "I Want to Get Old"

I used to think I'd be dead when I'm thirty,
Watching years go by so fast.
Used-up tracks, my arms are so dirty,
Now I think I just might have a chance.

Believing that I was Christ himself,
Galloping horse inside my veins.
Paranoid-schizoid, the doctors all tell me,
"Don't you think, boy, it's time for a change?"

If you want to get old—Lord, I want to get old.
I want to live again. I want to rock 'n' roll with you!

Married life is driving me crazy. In-laws say, he's not my kin.
Papa says, "Give me the knife; I'll carve up the baby.
You're daddy's little girl; you got to get away from him."

Twenty-one days I'm living a nightmare,
Losing my wife and my nine-to-five.
Give me a break—I think I deserve it.
You said we're to live; now I'm trying to keep that feeling alive.

I want to get old. Lord I want to get old.
I want to live again. I want to rock 'n' roll with you!

# ABOUT THE AUTHOR

B ORN IN A LOWER-MIDDLE-CLASS SECTION OF NEW York City in 1954, Sean Harrison has been called "The man of a million stories." After a successful thirty-two-year career in Orthopedics and raising a family, Sean has dedicated his life to the service of others. He is a community activist who believes addiction, and not money, is the root of all evil. He often is found sharing a meal with one of his "outdoor friends" or speaking to groups of men and women locked behind bars, in detox centers, and recovery houses throughout San Diego.

Sean's fundamental belief is that anyone who suffers from the pain of living can change the way they live by altering their thoughts. He inspires men and women from all walks of life, and his talks have mesmerized audiences for decades. In *Out of the Ghetto*, Sean shares a lifetime of insights about the horrors of addiction and the joys of recovery in a way that is lite and easy to understand.